God's Servants to Help Us Take Our Territory

angels
in our
territory

Graeme **Wylie**

Published by
Maurice Wylie Media
Your Inspirational Christian Publisher

Publishers' statement: Throughout this book the love for our God is such that whenever we refer to Him, we honour with Capitals. On the other hand, when referring to the devil, we refuse to acknowledge him with any honour to the point of violating grammatical rule and withholding capitalisation.

For more information visit
www.MauriceWylieMedia.com

Contents

Acknowledgements

I want to thank all who have helped me bring this book to the place of publication. I want to thank my wife Frances for reading and re-reading it with a fine-tooth comb, and for her constant love and support. I want to thank Judith Ferraro for checking the text and for helpful ideas and encouragement. Thanks to Eric Pechin for designing the cover and motivating me to write this book in the first place. Thanks to Gary Davidson for writing the foreword and to Alain Caron for his encouragement and helpful suggestions.

Dedication

I dedicate this book to Yahweh Sebaot, the Lord of hosts. Each of God's names and titles gives us a revelation about who he is and what he does. The word *"hosts"* is used in Scripture in two main ways.

Firstly it refers in the singular to the *"starry host"* those millions of billions of trillions of stars whom their Creator *"brings out one by one calling them each by name"* Isaiah 40:26. Astronomy reveals increasingly the magnitude and glory of the universe with its star-filled galaxies. We are now told that there are as many stars in the sky as there are grains of sand on all the seashores of the earth put together! How amazing and awesome is the God who is Lord of all this glorious host which functions at His command! Since the photographs coming from the Hubble telescope show an awesome spectacle of glorious wonder, how much more glorious and awesome is their Creator, the Lord of hosts!

Secondly, and more significantly, the hosts of whom Yahweh is the Lord are the hosts of angels, His heavenly entourage filling the courts of the universe. In the book of Revelation stars are a symbol of angels. Perhaps the number of angels in God's heavenly army is comparable to the numbers of stars. And surely the glory of these "glorious ones" is greater than the glory of the stars and also reflects something of the glory of their Creator too! The Lord and His angelic hosts keep the whole universe, with the sad exception of the rebellious earth, functioning fully in God's order and displaying His glory and majesty, wisdom and power.

Even the earth, despite being ravaged by sin, sickness, war and want because of man's rebellion, still displays much of its Creator's glory in beautiful scenery and glorious sunsets. The battle to reclaim it and renew it to its original splendour is well under way. David was one of those men after God's heart whose eyes were filled with what could be rather than what was. When his natural eyes saw a giant and an army of Philistine idol worshippers oppressing the people of God, his spiritual eyes saw the Lord of angelic hosts in whose presence he spent so much of his time.

'Then David said to the Philistine, "You come to me with a sword, with a spear, and with a javelin. But I come to you in the name of the LORD of hosts, the God of the armies of Israel, whom you have defied. This day the LORD will deliver you into my hand, and I will strike you and take your head from you. And this day I will give the carcasses of the camp of the Philistines to the birds of the air and the wild beasts of the earth, that all the earth may know that there is a God in Israel. Then all this assembly shall know that the LORD does not save with sword and spear; for the battle is the LORD's, and He will give you into our hands."
1 Samuel 17:45-47 (NKJV)

In the battles that we face today, despite all the forces of evil we see around us, may we have our eyes fixed on the Lord of hosts who is with us. May our vision of Him in His glory include the vision of His heavenly army whom He mobilises on our behalf to minister to us and fight for us!

Endorsements

"This is a highly original book, scriptural and well argued. An eye opening comment on the link between Christian responsibility to share the gospel and the ministry of angels serving the great purposes of God. Highly recommended."

Stuart Bell Senior Pastor of Alive Church and leader of the Ground Level Network — UK

"As I read this fascinating little book I thought that the author Graeme Wylie has the Caleb spirit. ("...*my servant Caleb has a different spirit and follows me wholeheartedly,"* Numbers 14:24)

He follows the Lord wholeheartedly. There are no half measures. He has a passion for God's Kingdom purposes. He is pressing on. There is more land to be gained. There is so much more for those who follow hard after the Lord.

We have much to learn from both the life of the author and his wife, and the message of this book. He longs to see God at work in our generation and he has a special God-given compassion for the people of Ireland and France.

Like the Apostle Paul he recognises that we do not wrestle against flesh and blood but against principalities and powers. His belief in the important ministry of angels is compelling and will bring fresh insights. In many ways this is a 'behind-the-scenes' book to where the action really is.

This generation desperately needs people with 'a different spirit.' Christians are called to be those people. This book will help us on that exciting Christ-centred Spirit-filled journey."

Bishop Ken Clarke Church of Ireland - Anglican Communion

"I have known Graeme for over 35 years and throughout his ministry he has shown himself to be an anointed leader of great personal integrity, passion for God, persevering faith and sacrificial obedience. 'Angels in our Territory' is both a timely and necessary contribution to the study of angels and their positive role in advancing God's kingdom in the world. Graeme presents a thoroughly biblical argument rooted in sound ministry experience of how angels are working with and on behalf of the people of God in bringing His rule and will to this earth. This book is written in a clear easy to read style and once I started reading I couldn't put it down. It is both inspiring and encouraging and I would strongly recommend this resource to every believer who is seeking for spiritual breakthrough in their sphere of work and ministry."

John McEvoy Director of Elim Ministries Ireland

"We count it an honour to write this short endorsement. Graeme is an anointed bible teacher and we have been privileged to sit under his ministry on many occasions. It has now become evident that the anointing also flows through him as he puts pen to paper.

Graeme has that wonderful gift of being real without being boring and being exciting without being extreme. Through this book he has brought us clear biblical teaching on this subject interlaced with real life accounts from his own journey as he and Frances have served God over these many years both in Ireland and in France. As you read these pages you will find fresh nuggets of revelation and a deeper desire for the living God who created these wonderful beings."

Robert & Rosemary McAuley Inspire Ministries — Ireland

Foreword

I have just finished reading the manuscript for *"Angels in our territory."*

I was greatly encouraged and challenged reading the "adventure"of Graeme and Frances! The Wylies arrived in Galway, Ireland in 1980, the same year that our family arrived in Dublin. We all had received a sovereign call to Ireland and by God's grace have seen Him honour our labour by raising up Spirit-filled churches the length and breadth of the nation.

This short pithy narrative is well written and filled with applicable spiritual principles. I was especially taken with references to the Huguenot movement, which I have studied with increasing interest over the years. It would seem to me that God puts "spiritual markers" down and we simply take up what has fallen in the past. We soon discover that God has a continuity within His plan and has been at work through the centuries.

It is refreshing to read of divine encounters with spiritual beings and to know, in a world which seems to have a fixation with evil, that God's children are not bereft of visitations by His messengers. There is a "holy fire" that burns in the breast of Graeme and Frances. I pray that fire will ignite in a new generation of believers for our nation and the world!

Gary Davidson
Founding pastor of St Mark's Church, Dublin and the Assemblies of God Ireland (AGI) network of churches and ministries.

Introduction

The concept of taking territory is a prominent one in Scripture. Adam was given a piece of territory on planet earth. It was a veritable Paradise providing an ideal and pleasing environment in which to prosper, till he forfeited it by following his own wisdom rather than God's.

God gave Israel a *"land flowing with milk and honey"*. He assigned that particular part of the planet to them as a people. But they had to take it, occupy it and cultivate it, because, since Adam's rebellion, the earth was now in hostile hands. It would require a battle, much sweat, hard work and determination to lay hold of all that God had promised them. But with faith in God, obedience to His directions and trusting His wisdom rather than their own, they could live a life of fulfilment where their work would be blessed and rewarded. God's ideal was that everyone would be secure and provided for in that territory. The utopian picture of peace and plenty painted by the prophets was that of *"every man under his own vine and his own fig tree"*. Fulfilment, provision and peace.

The analogy of Israel taking their physical territory is used in the New Testament as a picture of followers of Christ advancing the kingdom of God in every aspect of human society. Working together with God in a hostile environment, we defeat the usurper, liberate the captives, transform lives and society till the *"earth is filled with the glory of God as the waters cover the sea"*. Because of what Christ has done in defeating satan at the cross, we work with God to liberate the planet from satanic and moral pollution and restore it to its rightful King. The climax of the story will come when Christ returns and Paradise is restored in the new heaven and new earth. Then righteousness, peace and prosperity will reign for ever.

Each of us has a part to play in this great drama which is being enacted in human history. We find our life purpose, fulfilment and satisfaction when we each take the territory assigned to us, and advance the influence of the kingdom of God within our sphere of influence. We have an exciting mission to fulfil! This is what we exist for and what makes us tick. Fulfilling this mission aligns us with our Maker's design.

On the macro scale God gives some people a vision to see a city, a people group or a nation transformed by the power of the Gospel. On the micro scale God envisions others to make a significant impact for the kingdom of God among needy people in their community.

Robert and Rosemary have worked among mutually hostile paramilitaries in Northern Ireland to see their lives transformed and reconciled by the power of Christ. Mary leads a vision in Kilkenny to host a place where people can come and chat over free coffee and find support in life's struggles. Pauline and her team of volunteers provide free meals for hungry, lonely people in Arklow. Seamus has opened Healing Rooms in Carlow and the miracles God has done have made front page news in the local newspaper.

Linda has a vision to open a place in Athlone where lonely people can be connected and programmes can be run to facilitate mental health and wellbeing. John and Andy visit people in prison. Countless others around Ireland and all over the world have found their destiny in life in taking the territory God has assigned to them to advance the kingdom of God in their sphere of influence.

When God gives us a territory to take, whether on the macro or micro scale, he also sends an angel to lead, guide, and protect us, and to help us to deal with the enemies that oppose us. This book is about the discovery of this reality - about angels assigned to help us to take our territory. The challenges that face us may be many, but with the help of God and His ministering angels we can all make a difference in our world and find great joy in the process.

"See, I am sending an angel ahead of you to guard you along the way and to bring you to the place I have prepared."
Exodus 23:20

CHAPTER 1

Angels on Aeroplane Wings

We had just boarded our plane at Dublin airport on our journey to France on another mission trip. As we were settling in to our seats and buckling up our belts I suddenly sensed an awareness that was quite new to me. I found myself saying to Frances, my wife, that I sensed the presence of three angels on each wing of the aeroplane. I didn't see anything unusual; certainly I didn't see any angels. It was just a kind of *"knowing"* in the Spirit, like when one gets a *"word of knowledge"* or a prophetic word from the Lord.

I had always considered myself to be a *"feet on the ground"* type of conservative person theologically. I was an engineer by training and somewhat suspicious of people who were always *"seeing"* angels or demons although I believed firmly in the reality of the spirit realm. I had read with interest Billy Graham's excellent book, *"Angels, God's Secret Agents"* many years previously. I was impressed with his thoroughly biblical exposition on the topic of angels and their role in God's plan, as well as the many contemporary examples of everyday angelic activity which he had recounted. But it seemed to me that it was rather exceptional to be actually aware of their presence and activity. I believed in a general sense that, *"The angel of the Lord encamps around those who fear Him"*, but expected that we would probably only find out in heaven about actual cases where the angel may have intervened on our behalf. I didn't really expect that I would become aware of angelic activity in my life and ministry. Certainly in the previous forty years of ministry it had not been a prominent feature.

However, about a year or so previous to this experience on the aeroplane, when we felt God stirring us to begin exploring the possibility of ministry in France, we unwittingly found ourselves thrust into a new awareness of the angelic realm. A couple of our neighbours in Ireland, who had recently come to the Lord decided to move to France. My wife had been caring for them spiritually and felt that God said to her that her assignment with them wasn't finished yet. So we felt God prompting us to go and see them and try to find a church to link them with.

Frances felt God gave her the word God had given to Moses in Exodus 23:20 *"See, I am sending an angel ahead of you to guard you along the way and to bring you to the place I have prepared"*. That was a good encouragement to us, and I took it to mean that God would bring us there and back safely and our mission would be successful. But I didn't expect either to see or to sense the presence of the angel assigned to us. However, as we were leaving and had started to drive away from our home, Frances sensed the great joy of the angels who were accompanying us. They were so happy that we were going.

Then, after we had landed and were starting out on our journey in our hired car, Frances said, *"The angels are joyful that we are here"*. She really had this sense of the angels rejoicing that we had come to the land. I felt happy to be there in a beautiful location on a lovely spring day in the South of France away from the cloud and rain in Ireland. But her awareness of the angels was more sensitive than mine. I always considered her to be more prophetic and more sensitive to the spirit realm than me. God usually spoke to me through the Word and I rejoiced in knowing him intimately primarily through the Spirit and the Word together. Frances would hear God speaking to her about all sorts of things or people, directly into her spirit, while in prayer or doing the housework. But things were about to change for me as we embarked on this new adventure in scouting out the territory of France.

Our mission to find an English-speaking church for our friends was successful, but we also discovered that God had something else in mind for us too. I found that when we were in the land of France, the Spirit of God began tugging at my heart, and as we toured around the region over that weekend I felt as if the Spirit was assigning a new territory for me, a new sphere of ministry. Only later did I perceive that the territorial angels in the land were happy that we were there, because they were excited that God was stirring us to come to their territory. But that revelation was to come later.

Four months after that first exploratory visit, we came on a prophetic prayer journey. Diane Hill, a prophetic worshipper and intercessor in one of our family of churches in Ireland, had heard God tell her to mark the cross on France. So in obedience she gathered a team of prophetic worshippers and intercessors from our Irish churches and did the North to South leg from Calais to Perpignan that summer, and the West to East leg from Brest to Strasbourg the following summer. We joined in for the southern part of the first leg.

It was a real battle for us to go because our youngest son was in hospital. He was seriously ill and was losing blood and had collapsed while waiting in the emergency department to be examined. He was under observation and undergoing tests but had not yet been diagnosed. Should we, as responsible parents, leave him or should we stay and look after him? It was one of those difficult decisions and we felt there was a spiritual conflict going on in the wider picture. In the end, in consultation with him, we decided to go, but only for a few days. We cancelled the planned holiday with friends which we were to have afterwards while in France.

However, as soon as we arrived in France, and were on our journey in our hired car, around the same place where Frances felt the angels rejoicing on our previous visit, we got a phone call from our son in the hospital. The doctors had given him a preliminary diagnosis. Our hearts sank when he mentioned the name of the condition, as it was a lifelong incurable illness and represented our worst fears from the symptoms he had presented with. It was with a heavy heart that we continued our journey to join the rest of the team. But we chose to set that aside, with some difficulty, and focus on prayer for the region, listening to God and declaring the Word of the Lord.

Thankfully, the subsequent test results did not confirm the preliminary diagnosis and he was out of hospital by the time we got home. We have discovered through the years that not everything is plain sailing when we set out to follow the Lord. We are in a spiritual battle. When we step out in obedience to God the angels are happy but the devil is not. It is a fight of faith, and obedience to God is crucial if we are to be people of God's kingdom.

A 21 Day Assignment

While on that trip the Lord put it on our hearts that He had a 21 day assignment for us to fulfil the following month in France. So I prayed, *"Lord if you have a 21 day assignment for us then provide a house for us free of charge for 3 weeks so that we can fulfil our assignment in this region".* God answered that prayer very quickly and in a few days someone who didn't know us provided a lovely house for us in the beautiful Minervois region of the Languedoc, in the South of France. We still don't know that person and have never met him, but the free use of his house was a blessing to us. When we were there our attention was drawn to Deuteronomy 1:33 and God's reminder to Israel that He was the God *"who went ahead of you on your journey, in fire by night and in a cloud by day,* **to search out places for you to camp** *and to show you the way you should go."* God takes great care to send His messengers ahead of us to prepare places for us to stay as we take steps of obedience to follow him.

That proved to be an amazing 3 weeks. We had felt to spend that time a bit like Daniel fasting and praying for revelation and understanding of what was going on in that territory in the spirit realm. But before we had even got established in the house, I had just got my mobile phone connected to a French network when I got a phone call from a French man whom I had never met. We had briefly met his wife and daughters when we were in Perpignan the previous month *"marking the cross"* on France. He felt prompted by the Holy Spirit, and his wife, to phone us and invite us to come to Perpignan the following day. It was the concluding day of a week of prayer and fasting being held in their church, which was over an hour away. We felt this invitation was from God and thus began what became a significant relationship with the prophetic Pechin family who, at one level, opened the spiritual doors for us to minister in France.

"The fresh understanding I was receiving through these Scriptures was that there is a particular category of angels, or mighty ones, glorious ones who had territorial assignments and were attached to specific lands, nations and peoples."

CHAPTER 2

Territorial Angels in Scripture

We felt that God had truly gone ahead of us and prepared the way in some extraordinary ways during that entire 21 day period. Perhaps the most significant thing was that He began to open the Scriptures to me and give me new insights as we waited on him for revelation.

David and the Angels in the Land

My attention was drawn to Psalm 16 and particularly to verse 3 which in the NIV states, *"As for the saints [**holy ones**] who are in the land, they are the **glorious ones** in whom is all my delight"*. I had always thought that David was using the word *"saints"* in the same way that it is used in the New Testament to refer to God's holy people. But that meaning didn't quite seem to fit the context so I began to probe a bit deeper. I discovered that the Hebrew word translated *"saints"* was *"qadoshim"*, not *"hasidim"* the word usually translated saints. Derek Kidner, in the Tyndale Old Testament Commentary on the Psalms, says, "This word (qadoshim) is used in the Old Testament more often of heavenly beings than earthly ones." It is used to refer to angels as *"holy ones"* as in Psalm 89:5-7.

*'The heavens praise your wonders, LORD, your faithfulness too, in the assembly of the **holy ones**. For who in the skies above can compare with the LORD? Who is like the LORD among the **heavenly beings?** In the **council of the holy ones** God is greatly feared; he is more awesome than all who surround him.'* (NIV)

Here the Psalmist is clearly referring to the assembly of the holy ones in the skies above, to *"heavenly beings"*, to the council of holy ones in which God is seated as the Supreme Holy One. He is describing God enthroned as King in the midst of His royal entourage of angelic beings. David is describing how superior God is to these heavenly beings. He is more awesome than all who surround him and greatly feared by them, in the heavenly corridors of power.

The same picture is used in Deuteronomy 33:2

*'The LORD came from Sinai and dawned over them from Seir; he shone forth from Mount Paran. He came with **myriads of holy ones** from the south, from his mountain slopes.'* (NIV)

Moses and His Understanding of Angels for Nations
In the context, Moses is blessing the tribes of Israel just before he dies and he describes in poetic terms how God came with His people from Sinai to lead them into the territory He had assigned to them. He had guided them by a pillar of cloud by day and a pillar of fire by night, but as well, He Himself had overshadowed them and accompanied them with His heavenly retinue comprising thousands upon thousands of angels.

When an earthly monarch is on a state visit there is always a significant retinue of court officials and royal pomp and splendour. The pageantry of such occasions is proportional to the greatness of the monarch and the significance of the occasion. Royal occasions of state in England are always great displays of pageantry as Queen Elizabeth sets out with pomp and splendour. Sometimes she is in a gold carriage pulled by 8 splendid horses and accompanied by footmen, guards, the royal family and hosts of officials. Her entourage is designed to display wealth, grandeur and splendour to show the glory of her kingdom and status of her monarchy. Thus when God, the King of the universe, appeared on Mount Sinai to speak to the nation of Israel he did so with a fearful display of majesty and splendour with thunder, lightning, earth trembling, smoke and fire, as well as the heavenly retinue of angels with trumpet sound.

So when God was leading Israel to take their assigned territory it was an event of huge cosmic significance, involving heaven and earth cooperating to bring a manifestation of heaven to earth. Moses was more aware of the heavenly dimension than the people he was leading. They were still so earthbound in their vision that they grumbled and complained against Moses for 40 years. The only reason Moses had the grace and patience to persevere, according to Hebrews 11:27 was that *"he persevered because he saw him who is invisible".*

Moses had his eyes opened to the invisible realm. Although he had to lead a few million recalcitrant and obstinate humans he knew that he was accompanied by Almighty God and several millions of angels of varying functions and ranks. How important it is for leaders to have a heavenly vision, to see into the spirit realm, in order to persevere when everything in the earth realm seems to oppose at times as well as the dark spiritual forces.

This seems to be especially the case when it comes to taking our assigned territory for God. J. A. Thompson, in his commentary on Deuteronomy, [Tyndale Old Testament Commentaries, IVP, p307] gives an alternative translation of Deuteronomy verses 2 and 3.

*"With him were myriads of **holy ones**, At his right hand proceeded the **mighty ones**. Yea, the **guardians of the peoples**, All the holy ones are at thy hand. They prostrate themselves at thy feet, They carry out thy decisions".*

Thompson comments, *"Such a proposal represents Yahweh coming to Israel's aid accompanied by the heavenly host of holy ones and mighty ones who have the **care of the nations in their hands**"* [ibid]. He makes a distinction between the general hosts of holy angels and a particular contingent of mighty angels to whom have been assigned roles as guardians over specific nations or peoples.

In the previous chapter, in his poetic song which he recited to the whole nation of Israel shortly before his death, Moses gave further insight into his understanding of the role of angels in relation to the various nations and their territories. Deuteronomy 32:8-9.

"When the Most High gave the nations their inheritance, when he divided all mankind, he set up boundaries for the peoples according to the number of the sons of Israel. For the LORD's portion is his people, Jacob his allotted inheritance." (NIV)

The expression "the sons of Israel" is translated "the sons of God" in many manuscripts. This is a term frequently used in the Old Testament to refer to angels. God is referred to as "the Father of spirits" in Hebrews 12:9. This verse primarily refers to the fact that he is our Father because we are essentially spirit beings whom He has created. But God is the Father of all creation and angels are also spirits [Hebrews 1:14] whom He has created, so in this sense they can also be described as sons of God.

The Septuagint was the Greek version of the Old Testament frequently quoted by the writers of the New Testament in its original Greek. F. F. Bruce in his commentary [New International Commentary New Testament, The Epistle to the Hebrews, Eerdmans, p33] on Hebrews 2:5 says, *"To angelic beings the present world has been entrusted for administration, but not so the world to come".* The biblical evidence for the angelic government of the world is early: it goes back to the song of Moses in Deuteromy 32. The Septuagint reading of Deuteromy 32:8 [which claims to represent the original text] runs thus:

"When the Most High gave to the nations their inheritance,
When he separated the children of men, He set the bounds
of the peoples according to the number of the angels of God"

F. F. Bruce continues, **"This reading implies that the administration of the various nations have been parcelled out among a corresponding number of angelic powers**. " [ibid]

As for Israel, Moses states *"For the Lord's portion is his people, Jacob his allotted inheritance."* [Deuteronomy 32:9]. Later Daniel reveals that God has assigned Michael the archangel as the specific Guardian for the nation of Israel. [Daniel 10:20; 12:21]. As an archangel Michael was a ruler-angel with authority over a contingent of angels. He was one of the *"Mighty Ones"* who together with those under his control were assigned to the territory and people of Israel.

David's Delight in the Angels in His Territory

Returning to Psalm 16; that understanding throws new light on David's awareness of the spiritual powers at work in his kingdom. In verses 5 and 6 he is referring to the territory God has assigned to him:

*"LORD, you alone are my portion and my cup; you make **my lot** secure. The **boundary lines** have fallen for me in pleasant **places**; surely I have a **delightful inheritance**."* (NIV)

David's heart is for God Himself more than for any other inheritance God had apportioned to him. In Psalm 27:4 he says

*"**One thing** I ask from the LORD, **this only** do I seek: that I may dwell in the house of the LORD all the days of my life, **to gaze on** the beauty of the LORD and to **seek him** in his temple."* (NIV)

David was single minded in his pursuit of God. He was a true worshipper whose heart was captured by God. God meant more to him than anything else in life. His lifelong ambition was to gaze upon the beauty of the Lord and to seek Him in His temple. God was his priority, and if God never gave him any other inheritance he was satisfied with the Lord as his portion and inheritance.

To such a person, a man after God's own heart, God could entrust the care and leadership of His people on earth. So God gave David a territorial inheritance - God's own land, watched over by Michael the archangel and His hosts of guardian angels. David exults in this delightful inheritance which God has made secure and which His angels are guarding. The boundaries of David's kingdom were for the first time in Israel's history the original boundaries which God had assigned to His people.

David was the first person to realise the full extent of territory that God had assigned to Israel as a nation. He had understood some vital keys to taking his assigned territory.

24/7 Prayer and Praise

God had given him the revelation of the 24/7 tent of continual praise and worship to establish the throne of God in the land. And as well as taking his full delight in God himself, Psalm 16 verse 3 indicates that:

*"As for the **holy ones** who dwell in the land,*
*They are the **glorious ones** in whom is all my delight".*

David realised that the security of his country was not dependant on his good administration or on his armed forces, his military prowess or good government. All of those human aspects of nationhood were important but they were only successful because, through his spiritual pursuit of God and the centrality of a throne for Him on the praises of his people, the angelic forces were empowered to fulfil the totality of their mandate. They were the unseen guardians and administrators of God's purposes in the land. They were holy and glorious ones, and David took great delight in their role in enabling him to fulfil his territorial mandate. Hebrews 1:14 informs us that the angels are ministering spirits in God's service to serve the heirs of salvation.

Various Categories of Angels

There are all types of angels with different missions and functions. There are guardian angels around each individual believer with an assignment to protect. [Psalm 34:7]. Little children have their own angels who behold the face of their Father in heaven. [Matthew 18:10]. There are messenger angels sent on a specific commission to deliver a message on God's behalf, as Gabriel did to Mary. [Luke 1:26f]. There are angels sent to guide and give success in mission. [Genesis 24:7].

There are warrior angels [Revelation 12:7], angels who bring revelation [Revelation 1:1], strengthening angels [Luke 22:43] and delivering angels eg. Peter from prison [Acts 12:7f]. There are angels for virtually every function that God exercises in our favour. They are God's servants who do his bidding to help us in every way we need divine help. [Psalm 103:20]

The fresh understanding I was receiving through these Scriptures was that there is a particular category of angels, or *"mighty ones"*, or *"glorious ones"* who had territorial assignments and were attached to specific lands, nations and peoples.

Ps 34v7   Guardian Angels
" The angel of the Lord stooped down to listen as I prayed, encircling me, empowering me, + showing me how to escape - He will do this for everyone who fears God!"
" Be careful that you do not corrupt these little ones. For I assure you that in heaven each of their Angelic Guardians have instant access to my Heavenly Father" Matt 18v10
Luke 1v26 - Messenger Angels
" The Angel Gabriel was sent from God's presence to an unmarried girl named Mary... v31 You will become pregnant with a baby boy + you are to name him Jesus"
Gen 24v7 - Angels sent to guide + give success
" I will give you this 'Land' he (God) will send His angel before you so that you can get your son's wife from here"

"I began to discern that, in the region to which God was sending me, there needed to be the calling forth and raising up of generals in that territory to plant churches with an apostolic mandate to bring an incarnation of the kingdom of heaven to the region."

CHAPTER 3

Angels, Evangelism and Revival

Paul had a clear understanding that every nation was assigned its exact geographical place or territory by God and the duration of time for their assignment. Acts 17:26-27.

*'From one man he made all the nations, that they should inhabit the whole earth; and **he marked out their appointed times in history** and the **boundaries of their lands**. God did this so that they would seek him and perhaps reach out for him and find him, though he is not far from any one of us.'*

And, as we have seen, he has assigned territorial angels to these nations and their territory. Paul explains God's reasons for acting this way: it was so that, as a specific people group with their various national characteristics and those of their territory, they would seek God. Through the presence of God's angels in the land, He was not far from any one of them [v27]. The angels are there, positioned in the land, to help and assist those who rise up to take the land through the preaching of the Gospel. When the Gospel is proclaimed in the power and demonstration of the Spirit the kingdom of God is *"at hand"* [Matthew 4:17-25]. God's purpose was that all the nations would come to the knowledge of God. His strategies for manifesting the kingdom of heaven on earth were centred on national territories and people groups.

The Angels and People-Group Evangelism

The angels are integrally involved in this process of evangelising nations and people groups, since they are *"ministering spirits sent forth to minister to the heirs of salvation"* [Hebrews 1:14]. While the mandate of angels is not the preaching of the Gospel, [that is our mandate] they are integrally involved in facilitating the preaching of the Gospel and the reception of the message. Sometimes there is a tendency to focus more on the demonic powers which frustrate and hinder the preaching of the Gospel and seek to prevent people from coming to know the Lord. That focus can undermine our faith and expectation, and may instead empower the enemy by acknowledging him. It is much better to acknowledge Scriptural teaching about the positive role and involvement of His angelic agents in this process and thus activate our faith and expectation of God.

The initial mission of Jesus was specifically to the *"lost sheep of the house of Israel"* [Matthew 10:6]. When he sent His disciples out on their initial mission it was to this people group, and they were expressly forbidden to go to the Gentiles or Samaritans at that season. God works with specific people groups in specific seasons. Later, when he gave them the great commission in Matthew 28:19- 20 he expanded the territorial spheres to which they were sent, but they were still to focus on discipling nations.

*'Therefore go and make **disciples of all nations**, baptising them in the name of the Father and of the Son and of the Holy Spirit, and teaching them to obey everything I have commanded you. And surely I am with you always, to the very end of the age.'*

The concept inherent in this verse is that they were to make disciples *of* each people group, not just make disciples *in* all the nations. Likewise in Acts 1:8 their mandate was one of increasing geographic and territorial spread beginning at Jerusalem and extending to the ends of the earth.

*'But you will receive power when the Holy Spirit comes on you; and you will be my witnesses in **Jerusalem**, and in **all Judea** and **Samaria**, and to **the ends of the earth**.' (*NIVUK)

Territorial Revivals

In the early 5th century, around 432AD, a Roman Briton was called to cross the Irish Sea from Britain to Ireland to bring the Gospel to the Irish. He had previously been a slave herding pigs for about 6 years after he had been captured on a raid to Britain and taken to Ireland. He escaped from his captors and went back to Britain, where he remained for some time.

'Then I saw in the night a vision of a man, whose name was Victoricus, coming as it were from Ireland, with countless letters. And he gave me one of them and I read the opening words of the letter which were, 'The voice of the Irish': and as I read the beginning of the letter I thought that at the same moment I heard their voice.. and thus did they cry as with one mouth: 'We ask thee boy, come and walk among us once more.' And I was quite broken in heart and could read no further, and so I woke up.'
— Confessions of St. Patrick

In all probability, Victoricus was an angel who communicated this call of God to go to the Irish people with the Gospel. Patrick set out in obedience and for the next 30 years evangelised Ireland so effectively that the nation was converted from Druidism to Christianity in one generation. St Patrick's ministry was accompanied with signs and wonders and he has rightly become known as the Apostle to Ireland.

Throughout the history of revivals when God has sovereignly poured out His Spirit and brought great numbers into the kingdom of God it has usually been in territories and among people groups. For example, the Welsh revival of 1904, the East African revival in the 1950s, the Indonesian revival in the 1960s, the Ulster revival in 1859, the Huguenot revival in seventeenth century France and so on. And the spread of revival from these people groups usually went to other territories or people groups where there were particular connections. So we can see from Scripture and history that God's plan to bring in His kingdom from the heaven realm to the earth realm involves people groups and territories and that the territorial angels are particularly involved in this process. It was often during the heightened spiritual sensitivity at revival times that people became aware of unusual angelic activity.

Angels in the Cevennes

During the revival of the *"little prophets"* in the Cevennes in the Languedoc region of France during the late seventeenth century, there was great persecution and fierce opposition. People frequently heard angels singing Psalms, particularly where their churches had been demolished to prevent them from worshipping. The people believed that Jesus' statement in Luke 19:40 was relevant to this - that if the children who were praising God were to keep quiet *"the very stones would cry out in praise to God"*. Since they no longer had churches to worship God in, and were forbidden to do so in their homes under threat of arrest and possible death, God still was to be praised. The angels kept the worship going to secure the presence and ongoing action of God in the territory. [*"Le Réveil des Cévennes "*by Pierre Demaude].

As God was unfolding this understanding of the Scriptures to me during this 21 day assignment for revelation about the territory I was coming to, the Holy Spirit began to show me that there were still angels *"in the land"* of the Languedoc region of France. But many of them are waiting for the human generals of God's army, the church, to arise and act territorially to take the land in this generation.

God was showing me that these angels were *"in the land"* of France and in the Occitan region in particular, just as David became aware that there were *"holy ones in the land"* of his delightful inheritance assigned by God to his territory. [Psalm 16]. In the past I had been more cognizant of malevolent demonic spirits being attached to particular places of idolatry or places of gross iniquity and at times had felt that we should be pulling down these strongholds by our prayers and worship.

But now God was giving me a new more positive focus. Where land and territory had been dedicated to him historically and occupied by praising and worshipping believers in past generations, he still had his angels in occupation watching over their particular territory waiting for a new generation to arise and take that territory for the kingdom of heaven in their generation. The assignment and mandate of the territorial angels had not been withdrawn. So perhaps that is why we sensed the angels in the land rejoicing as soon as we had set our feet on their territory to seek God's purposes.

What was equally clear to me was that the mandate to evangelise and demonstrate the kingdom of God by preaching the Gospel, healing the sick and casting out devils was not given to angels but to believers.

'He said to them, "Go into all the world and preach the gospel to all creation. Whoever believes and is baptised will be saved, but whoever does not believe will be condemned. And these signs will accompany those who believe: in my name they will drive out demons; they will speak in new tongues; they will pick up snakes with their hands; and when they drink deadly poison, it will not hurt them at all; they will place their hands on people who are ill, and they will get well.' Mark 16:15-18

The supernatural manifestation of God's kingdom coming to the realm of men would only be realised as Spirit-empowered men and women obeyed their divine mandate. Angels would be on hand to help, but would not do man's part.

Apostolic and Angelic Collaboration

We see in Acts 10 that an angel appeared to Cornelius and gave him instructions to send for Peter, complete with address and postcode of where to find him! But the angel did not preach the Gospel to Cornelius. It was Peter who did that. Peter was listening to the Spirit's directions through a vision God had given him to prepare him for going to Cornelius.

Peter was just about to open the door to take a new territory for the kingdom - the Gentiles. Up till now he had been focussing on the Jews but it was a new season in the advance of the kingdom into another whole people group and probably the most significant step forward for the church in history. It would open the door of faith to all the non-Jewish nations of the world. God deployed His angelic messengers to work alongside His apostolic leader to begin to take this territory.

Peter and the other apostles had already been given their earth-taking mandate in general and global terms by Jesus. But the phased development of that in God's timing required revelation of what God was doing at that particular season. This came with revelatory vision, angelic coordination and the Spirit speaking to Peter. Then the Holy Spirit showed up in spectacular fashion to authenticate the work of God and show to disbelieving Jewish believers that it was actually God at work among the Gentiles. This was demonstrated by the miraculous gift of speaking in tongues as the people received the Word Peter preached.

So the involvement of angels in the advance of the kingdom is crucial, working alongside the human apostolic and evangelistic messengers. They clearly rejoice in their assignment and the opportunity they get to work alongside us in helping us to fulfil our mandate to take the territory God has assigned to us.

A modern day example of this was related to me some time ago. It concerned two Muslim men who went on a pilgrimage to Mecca.

While they were there they had an angelic visitation. The angel told them to go to Marseille in the South of France and gave them the particular address to go to and that there they would be told the truth. They were obviously sincere seekers of truth and they obeyed the angel's message. When they found the address and knocked on the door they told the story that they had been sent by an angel to that address to be told the truth. The astounded hosts were Christian missionaries to Muslims who lived at that address and were delighted to proclaim the truth about Jesus Christ! We live in an age when this sort of thing is happening frequently, particularly in many Muslim countries. God is using His angelic messenger to link up sincere seekers with His anointed servants.

A New Territorial Mandate

As I sought the Lord and He began to give me new insights into the Scriptures, I began to discern that, in the region to which God was sending me, there needed to be the calling forth and raising up of generals in that territory to plant churches with an apostolic mandate to bring an incarnation of the kingdom of heaven to the region. I felt that God was asking me to come alongside the French men and women God would raise up and thrust forth with this mandate to take their territory.

I had spent the previous 35 years taking the territory in Ireland that God had assigned to me in various phases, and now I was to support those who were to take their territory in this part of France and wherever God would send me. I felt a little bit like the two and a half tribes of Israel who had been assigned their territory east of the Jordan and had taken it already. But they were to leave their territory and go and help their brothers to take their territory West of the Jordan before settling down to enjoy their own territory.

During this time God spoke to me through Genesis 26 when God spoke to Isaac and told him, *"Live in the land where I tell you to live. Stay in this land for a while and I will be with you and will bless you."* I read it in my French Bible which says *"Séjourne dans ce pays-ci"* and I felt God specified ***"Séjourne dans ce pays-ci : le pays de l'Occitanie"***. I discovered that Occitanie was the former name given to a large part of the South of France where the Huguenots were largely based over 300 years ago. What I did not know then was that, in three years' time (2016) the name Occitanie would be revived for the new region formed by the merger of Languedoc - Roussillon and Midi-Pyrénèes. When that happened I was amazed that God had given me that name for the territory I was in, three years before the government did so!

So we gradually began to grasp a sense of God's unfolding plan for us in broad terms. This 21 day period of revelation opened for me a new understanding of how God wanted us to function in the next season of ministry and the importance of understanding the role of territorial angels.

I began to sense that God wanted to re-open the spiritual wells in that region that had been bursting with spiritual life in the past. God began to unpack Genesis 26 to me in a new way as a strategy to take this region. Some time later a French prophet whom I believe God is raising up as a general in the region, prophesied over me that this was our territory, that we had authority in France, and were not just visiting ministries with an open door here. But this is part of the territory God is giving us, since we have put our feet on the ground here. We would open wells of revival, wells of revelation and wells of healing in the land. That is what we are currently praying for.

"The terrorist attacks on France and the ongoing threat in Europe is all part of the wider scene in which God is setting the scene when divine activity will eclipse human evil."

CHAPTER 4

The Angels are Stirring

It was two years later before we eventually moved to live in France. During that time we made repeated visits for prayer in the land, to meet other pastors, and eventually to speak in various churches and conferences. We began to make plans to hand over our various responsibilities in Ireland and to transition the leadership of these ministries to others. And we were trying to sense the timing of God to make the move.

During this season, while we were worshipping the Lord at our annual leadership conference I sensed the Spirit say to me, *"The angels are stirring"*. Something that had been inactive in the spirit realm was beginning to stir in preparation for a new season of activity. It was time for us to put our plans for moving into operation in the season of God.

Kingdom Seasons

Scripture is very clear that there are seasons of kingdom activity. They often reflect the pattern of the earthly seasons. Winter is a time when things are dormant, not inactive. Important processes of rest and renewal and preparation take place in seasons when there is less overt activity. Spring brings the blossoming of new sprouts of life and growth. Things begin to warm up. New vision emerges. There is hope and excitement at the possibilities and one is energised to launch new initiatives.

Summer is a time when one is in the full flow of kingdom activity. Growth is continuing apace. Certain crops are harvested and others are awaiting fullness and ripeness. Then autumn brings in the full harvest. There is abundant fruitfulness and the joy of reaping what one had sown in the earlier seasons of life. But there can also be tiredness through long hours of toil to bring in the harvest and manage all the associated stresses and strains. One is ready for another winter season of rest, renewal and consolidation of the gains of the last season's growth.

The seasons don't change abruptly but gradually transition from one season to another. Sometimes there can be two separate seasons happening simultaneously. On the one hand, looking back over a lifetime of 44 years in ministry so far, I was in the autumn of life and, in the natural, I was approaching retirement age. But, in the spiritual realm, I was moving into a new spring season with fresh buds of revelation and a fresh call to new pastures. On one hand I was quite tired humanly speaking, having endeavoured to give my best in the previous 35 years church-planting in the Republic of Ireland. But on the other hand I was being rejuvenated with a fresh sense of excitement about a new assignment from the Lord. I had to manage both things going on simultaneously. This meant that I had to allow enough time to rest and be restored as well as prepare for the next phase. My wife, who was on the same journey with me, and going through similar experiences, had to help me to keep the equilibrium and pace myself accordingly. So the transition period took rather longer than I had initially anticipated. Thank God for a wise wife! Our first exploratory visit to France was in the spring time and the leaves were just coming out on the vines as we drove through the beautiful wine producing region of the Aude valley. Our third visit was in the autumn just at the beginning of the grape harvest. I felt the Lord saying to me, that just as our spring time of our ministry had been in France over 40 years ago when we had sown much and reaped little, so God was bringing us back to France for the autumn of our ministry so that we could participate in the harvest that God was going to bring in, in France in the next season. My heart wept and rejoiced at the prospect. I had spent my first 3 years of ministry in France as a young man. They were hard times, times of testing, times of physical pain and suffering, times of disappointment as we tried to share the Gospel again and again and again with people who were not in the slightest interested. Door after door shut in our faces, day after day, week after week, year after year.

I particularly remember one day in Cavaillon in Provence, after an afternoon of knocking on doors, when one particular door shut rather vehemently in our faces, I was overwhelmed with a feeling of rejection. I began to feel sorry for myself. I had given up a promising career as an engineer, turned down great financial offers to spend my time in a foreign country speaking a foreign language to share the Gospel with people who had no interest. The cold Mistral was blowing, it was a dark winter evening, hunger pangs were gnawing at my stomach as my ulcerous duodenum began to object to this lifestyle. Why did I have to suffer such repeated rejection?

And then it dawned on me. It wasn't me they were rejecting but the One who had sent me. Jesus was the *"despised and rejected of men."* I was to follow the example of the disciples who rejoiced that they were counted worthy to suffer for His name. I don't think I managed much rejoicing at that season. But now, 40 years later the Lord was promising me that I would be able to join in the harvest season in France. And a wave of joy overwhelmed me at the goodness of God for allowing me this privilege.

'Those who sow with tears will reap with songs of joy. Those who go out weeping, carrying seed to sow, will return with songs of joy, carrying sheaves with them.' Psalm 126:5-6

I enjoy the inestimable blessing and privilege of a godly inheritance. One of my frequent memories when I got up in the morning was of my father on his knees at the armchair in the kitchen. Often when he finished praying he would get up and start singing an old song:

> *"I will work for Jesus till the shadows fall,*
> *Labour for the Master till I hear his call.*
> *At the dewy evening, when the reapers leave,*
> *We will come rejoicing, bringing in the sheaves.*
> *Bringing in the sheaves, bringing in the sheaves,*
> *We will come rejoicing, bringing in the sheaves."*

As a farmer he knew all about the long seasons of toil, ploughing and harrowing the soil, sowing the seed, watching and waiting for the crop to grow and ripen. Only at the very, very end of the process was there any harvest. **The gain comes to those who persevere in the fields through till the end of harvest.** We live in days when people expect quick results or they get discouraged and give up. Perseverance till the end is important if we are to see the full harvest brought in.

'Jesus said to his disciples, Don't you have a saying, It's still four months until harvest? I tell you, open your eyes and look at the fields! They are ripe for harvest. Even now the one who reaps draws a wage and harvests a crop for eternal life, so that the sower and the reaper may be glad together. Thus the saying 'One sows and another reaps' is true. I sent you to reap what you have not worked for. Others have done the hard work, and you have reaped the benefits of their labour.' John 4:35-38.

I truly believe that, in the seasons of God, there is a new reaping to come in France. There is a rising longing for revival, for a new outpouring of the Holy Spirit and for a new generation of young people to be swept into the kingdom of God. France is ripe, the ground is being prepared. The terrorist attacks on Paris and the ongoing threat in Europe is all part of the wider scene in which God is setting the scene when divine activity will eclipse human evil.

God is shaking the nation and stirring the church to prayer. He is also raising up prayer in other nations for France. And He is positioning or repositioning key people for specific roles in the coming move of the Spirit.

France a Key Nation with a Unique Destiny
I believe that France is a very unique nation with a prophetic destiny in the purposes of God. When God moves in France, Europe will be affected and the French speaking world will be impacted. France was spiritually and economically impoverished when the Huguenots had to flee the country to other nations because of intense persecution. But they brought their gifts and skills to those nations, including Ireland, Britain, Holland, South Africa, America and others. It is time for those nations to bring a spiritual blessing back to France.

I was born and brought up in Northern Ireland where for many years the linen industry was the main industry. My father gained his income in his early years from growing flax for the linen industry. About 10,000 Huguenots fled to Ireland and it was the Huguenots who brought the finer skills and abilities to make high quality damask linen, which revolutionised the linen industry in Northern Ireland and brought much economic success.

In Lisburn alone there were hundreds of Huguenots who settled and left their blessing. There are now about 135 churches in the Lisburn area and many of the people are of Huguenot descent. I sense that it is time for the places and peoples who have been blessed directly or indirectly through the French people to bring their blessing to the French nation today. Paul taught the Gentile nations to bless the Jewish nation from which the blessing of the Messiah and the Gospel had come. It is time to bless France through prayer, through giving and through going to the nation with the love of God. The angels in France are stirring. And the Spirit was stirring me to recognise the time to go.

"It would seem that many of the functions that we look to God to perform for us, He actually does through his angels."

CHAPTER 5

Discerning the Presence and Functioning of Angels

I had been invited to speak in a church in Lisburn. The pastor was of one of those who were of Huguenot descent and his wife had died after a year long battle with cancer. He, his family and the whole church were grieving. She had been such an integral part of nearly everything that had happened in the church for thirty years that her loss was deeply felt. I was in France at the time of her death, but had returned to Ireland about a month later and really wanted to bring something from God to the church in their time of grief.

In the natural it was a difficult task to try and comfort a grieving congregation, but they were an important church for me and I was feeling a deep sense in my spirit that I wanted to be with them at that time and bring something from God. I had prepared a message in advance and, as I often do, I was preparing my spirit in prayer the night before, at times during the night, and in the morning on the 3 hour journey there. As I did so I realised that the message I had prepared earlier in the week was not sitting easily on my spirit. So I just cast myself on the Lord to inspire me as I spoke from my heart. I was conscious of a restfulness in my spirit and a real flow of anointing as I spoke, mainly from certain Scriptures in Job, without any notes. It just seemed that the words flowed easily and that the Spirit was resting on me. I felt God had given me a prophetic word for the church during the worship, which I shared as I spoke.

Afterwards a couple of people, who know me really well, including my wife, said that they had rarely heard me speak better. I knew I'd had divine help. Then a young girl told me that she had seen angels standing behind me as I spoke and she showed me what she had seen, as she had drawn it on her tablet. I was amazed. She was a prophetic young woman who had discerned something I had not discerned. I had always associated the anointing directly with the Holy Spirit. What I began to realise through this and other subsequent experiences was that angels may well be involved in communicating the Holy Spirit's help. The Holy Spirit is the *"Helper"* par excellence.

'I have spoken these things to you while staying with you. But the Helper — the Holy Spirit, Whom the Father will send in My name — that One will teach you all things, and remind you of everything which I said to you.' John 14:24-25 Disciples' Literal New Testament

The Holy Spirit is the *"Paracletos"* - *"the One called alongside"*, the *"Helper"* Jesus promised us. But Hebrews 1:14 tells us that angels are messengers in God's service to help us too. It seems that when God the Holy Spirit comes with help he also includes angels in the process of administering that help. They are in the service of the Spirit to mediate God's help to us. In the Old Testament when God gave the law to Israel we are told that, *"God spoke all these words"*; Exodus 20:1. But in the New Testament we have an increased insight through the Holy Spirit into the process God used. Hebrews 2:2 refers to the same situation and reveals that the message was spoken by angels.

*'For the **message God delivered through angels** has always stood firm...'*

Paul also states in Galatians 3:19 *'**God gave his law through angels** to Moses, who was the mediator between God and the people.'*

It would seem that many of the functions that we look to God to perform for us, He actually does through angels. It does not cease to be God who is doing it, but He does it through His agents. They represent him. They are His servants to help us. That is their designated function, but often we have not discerned their presence or functioning. This particular incident opened my eyes through the discernment of someone else who sensed or *"saw"* angels standing behind me right close up to me. I had sensed the anointing of the Holy Spirit in a more significant way than usual.

I have never yet seen angels with my natural vision, but I now expect to at some point. But I have begun to perceive the presence of angels. We may *"see"* them with the eyes of our spirit, even if we don't see them with our natural eyes.

One of the gifts of the Spirit is "discerning of spirits".
"For to one a word of wisdom is given through the Spirit; and to another, a word of knowledge according to the same Spirit; to a different one, faith by the same Spirit; and to another, gifts of healings by the one Spirit; and to another, things worked by miracles; and to another, prophecy; and to another, **discernments of spirits**; *to a different one, kinds of tongues; and to another, interpretation of tongues."*
Disciples' Literal New Testament - 1 Corinthians 12:8-10 [DLNT]

This gift works at various levels. It is interesting that the word *"discernments"* is plural in this literal translation from the Greek. This hints that there are various types of discernment relating to different aspects of the spirit realm. The discerning of evil spirits or unclean spirits is very helpful in deliverance ministry. Discerning whether a person is speaking by the Holy Spirit, by an evil spirit, or just by their own spirit is also important in deciding whether or not to give place to a particular utterance. But Hebrews 1:14 tells us that angels are also spirits. They are invisible spirit beings whom God has created.

'For in him all things were created: things in heaven and on earth, visible and invisible, whether thrones or powers or rulers or authorities; all things have been created through him and for him.' Colossians 1:16.

They may on occasion manifest themselves in visible form, at least to some who are present and not to others. Balaam's ass saw the angel but the prophet did not, when he should have done. [Numbers 22:21-33]. But his spiritual eyes were blinded by the hope of financial gain from his mission. He did not discern when God was actually using an angel to oppose him, because his motives were impure. This demonstrates both the importance of discerning the angelic in our ministry and the importance of pure hearts for the gift of discernment to be in operation. Our motives are so important for all the spiritual gifts. I believe that is why God sandwiched the two main chapters which speak about spiritual gifts, [chapters 12 and 14 of 1 Corinthians] around the great *"love chapter"* chapter 13.

'Follow the way of love and eagerly desire gifts of the Spirit, especially prophecy.' 1 Corinthians 14:1

Love for God and our fellow man is to be our highest aim. It is this passionate love that is to motivate us to seek the spiritual gifts we need at any particular time to express our loving service to God and our fellow man. Balaam needed the gift of discernment to see that he was prepared to misuse his prophetic gift for personal gain.

Co-Working with God and the Angels

God has called us to be co-workers with him. If we are to be His collaborators we need to be aware of what he is doing and how we are to collaborate. This involves being aware of the diverse ways in which he operates, and angels are such an integral part of His workforce. So I have begun to pray, *"Lord give me discernment of the presence and operation of angels to the degree that I need to be aware of what you are doing and how I am to co-operate with you. And keep me from seeing that which I don't need to see."*

We don't need any self-motivated desire for the spectacular or anything that puffs us up with pride, but purely that which facilitates us best serving God, worshipping him and collaborating with him.

On one of our early ministry trips to France, Frances and I were both struggling with our French and very aware of our clumsiness in expressing ourselves. We were spending a few days with our dear friends Elie and Judith Ferraro and asked them to pray with us about this specifically. As we were about to leave on our final morning with them, Judith came to deliver to us a number of *"words"* the Lord had given her. One of them was that an angel would be assigned to us to give us the right word at the right time. This was a great encouragement. We both spoke at a conference over the next few days and were aware of God's anointing on us as we spoke. Normally, when speaking in French, we are more dependent on our notes than when speaking in English. But, for the first time, I felt free to set my notes aside for a part of the message and speak without notes and did so with freedom. Then the following day I was speaking at another church in a different city and I spoke for 45 minutes completely without notes for the first time, as I felt the flow of the Holy Spirit giving me something to share which was not in my notes. Then I remembered Judith's words about the angel giving us the right words to say at the right time. Thank you Lord for your angel!

The Angels Bring Revelation

Revelation 10 is about an angel with a little scroll lying open in his hand. A voice tells John, *"Go, take the scroll that lies open in the hand of the angel who is standing on the sea and on the land." So I went to the angel and asked him to give me the little scroll. He said to me, "Take it and eat it. It will turn your stomach sour, but in your mouth it will be as sweet as honey."* I took the little scroll from the angel's hand and ate it. It tasted as sweet as honey in my mouth, but when I had eaten it, my stomach turned sour. Then I was told, *"You must prophesy again about many peoples, nations, languages and kings."* Revelation 10:8-11

An angel was involved in bringing to John the scroll with the message he was to prophesy. He was to digest the message himself, internalise it and sense the sweet and sour aspects of the message he was to deliver.

The whole book of Revelation was a revelation of Jesus Christ which was given to John by an angel, showing him what lay ahead. Revelation 1:1. *"The revelation from Jesus Christ, which God gave him to show his servants what must soon take place. He made it known by sending his angel to his servant John,"* [NIV]. The revelation was of Jesus, and was from Jesus, but it was mediated to John via an angel. We need revelation of what God is doing in the earth and in the territory he has assigned to us. So we need to have access to every means of revelation that God uses.

And we need revelation of the words God wants us to speak when we minister in His name. We need to internalise God's word deep inside ourselves and experience it at work in us before it can be effective through us. *"Lord, give us discernment of spirits to discern when your ministering spirits are present and operating with us, or on our behalf to help us fulfil more effectively the mandate you have given us."*

Writing the Revelation

In Jeremiah 36:1-2 we read:
Word came to Jeremiah from the LORD: "Take a scroll and write on it all the words I have spoken to you…"

We are not told how the word from the Lord came to Jeremiah, whether or not it was by an angel. We are not necessarily given everything through the mediation of angels, although that does seem to be one of their specific functions. But the writing down of divine revelation does seem to be important.

Habakkuk was also told to write,
"Write down the revelation and make it plain on tablets so that a herald may run with it. For the revelation awaits an appointed time; it speaks of the end and will not prove false. Though it linger, wait for it; it will certainly come and will not delay." Habakkuk 2:2-3. [NIVUK]

Over the last number of years God has told me at least 7 times through some very significant prophets that I am to write. But I have always prevaricated. What I have written in the past has always been hard work on my part and it hasn't always been published. But after a trusted prophet gave me a pen as a prophetic gift I made a definite commitment to start writing. I made several starts and stopped after a few pages as it just didn't seem to be flowing. Then one day, when urged by my friend Eric Pechin to write specifically about territorial angels, I asked him to lay hands on me and release the blockages that were holding me back. The Spirit did something as He came over me and I handed the keys of the car to my wife to drive home.

I sat down at the computer and within the next 24 hours I had written over 5000 words, which is not normal for me. As I have continued to write I have gradually become aware of angelic help. I have often said, *"I am a speaker, not a writer"*, but I have had to break those negative words off my life. As a result there has been a flow that has come in a whole new way, together with new revelation as I have been writing. But that doesn't eliminate all the hard work still involved in the whole writing and editing process!

"Thank you Lord for your angelic ministers! Give me growing discernment to see the various ways you are working with and through me."

A Warning

One of the things that concerns me, however, with the renewed awareness of angelic activity, is that certain people go around ordering angels to do this or do that. I do not see biblically that we have the authority to command angels to act in any given way. We certainly have *"authority over serpents and scorpions and over all the power of the enemy"*. Luke 10:19. We have authority over unclean spirits to cast them out. Luke 9:1 *"When Jesus had called the Twelve together, he gave them power and authority to drive out all demons and to cure diseases..."*

But nowhere in Scripture are we given such authority over angels. Even satan knew that when he quoted Psalm 91:11-12 to Jesus in Luke 4:10-11. For it is written: *"He will command his angels concerning you to guard you carefully; they will lift you up in their hands, so that you will not strike your foot against a stone."*

It is God who commands the angels because they are ***"his mighty ones who do his bidding, who obey his word"*** Psalm 103:20

Jesus as man, anointed by the Holy Spirit, did not have the authority to call angels.

"Do you think I cannot call on my Father, and he will at once put at my disposal more than twelve legions of angels?" Matthew 26:53

He would have to call on His Father to do so as the angels were subject to the Father's bidding. We do not have any more authority than the anointed Son of God when he was on earth. However, we can ask the Father to deploy His angels, since Jesus had the authority to do that and he has delegated that authority to us in the great commission. They are His servants; they serve us too as we serve God. But they are not our servants and we are not their master.

However, when God has given us His 'rhema' word to declare, the angels are listening for His word. They spring into action when they hear His word in our mouth proclaimed with the anointing and authority of the Holy Spirit. This is not a casual ordering of angels at our whim, but a collaboration with God that releases them to action.

"it was the role of the angels to engage the dark principalities, not Daniel's."

CHAPTER 6

Angels Assigned to our Territory

Territory is important. The English word *"territory"* comes from the same Latin root [terra] as the French word *"terre"*, meaning *"earth"*. *"The highest heavens belong to the Lord, but **the earth he has given to man**."* Psalm 115:16

The whole territory of the earth has been assigned to man and angels have been assigned to regions of the earth to help man fulfil his mandate to rule and exercise dominion over the earth. I believe that where evil men exercise wicked rule and domination, they open spiritual doors to give legitimate access to evil principalities and powers to their particular territory. When godly men rule they facilitate the angelic powers of good assigned to their territory.

Repeatedly through the Old Testament God reproaches backslidden Israel for defiling ***his land*** through their idolatry, immorality, divination and all sorts of evil.

*"But you came and **defiled my land** and made my inheritance detestable. The priests did not ask, 'Where is the LORD?' Those who deal with the law did not know me; the leaders rebelled against me. The prophets **prophesied by Baal, following worthless idols**."* Jeremiah 2:7-8.

"I will repay them double for their wickedness and their sin, because they have <u>defiled my land</u> with the lifeless forms of their vile images and have filled my inheritance with their detestable idols." Jeremiah 16:18

Wickedness defiles the land. The worship of other gods defiles the land. Paul makes clear that the worship of other gods is the worship of demons. *"The sacrifices of pagans are offered to demons, not to God."* 1 Corinthians 10:20 [NIV]. Since all human authority is ordained by God, those in governmental authority who engage in idolatrous worship, wickedness, injustice or corruption enable the powers of darkness over the territory where they rule. Thus a land or territory which legitimately belongs to God ["the earth is the Lord's" Ps 24:1], may come increasingly under the active control of the evil one. 1 John 5:19 *"The whole world lies under the control of the evil one."*

The Importance of Authorities

One of the priorities God gives us is to pray for is good government. *"I urge, then, **first of all**, that petitions, prayers, intercession and thanksgiving be made for all people – **for kings and all those in authority**, that we may live **peaceful and quiet lives in all godliness and holiness**. This is good, and pleases God our Saviour, **who wants all people to be saved and to come to a knowledge of the truth.**"* 1 Timothy 2:1-4

Those in authority impact the spiritual climate of their sphere of authority. The principal of a school is the main influence on the spiritual atmosphere of that school. The mayor of a city and the governing council affect the spiritual climate of that city. The governmental leaders or heads of state in any nation affect the spiritual climate of that nation. If there is corruption at any level in society it brings a sense of injustice which works against good government and good citizenship.

Paul instructs Timothy, concerning the churches for which he is responsible, to prioritise prayer for kings and all who are in authority. We should pray for good government which acts justly. *"Righteousness and justice are the foundation of your throne."* Psalm 89:14. God's throne is founded on righteousness and justice, so good human government should reflect that. Paul gives the reasons for praying for good government as twofold. Firstly, good and just government facilitates peace in society and godly living in the church. Secondly, it creates the climate in which there is freedom for evangelism, because God wants everyone to come to the knowledge of the truth. Repressive regimes throughout the world limit freedom of religion and oppress godly people.

Good government affects the spiritual atmosphere and limits evil powers. So people become more responsive to the Gospel.

A number of years ago, many intercessors in Ireland started to pray that corruption in high places would be exposed. During the last decade there has been a series of exposures of mass corruption in political circles, business circles, the banking sector and more recently in the police force. Child abuse in the institutional church has been exposed and the massive cover up which denied justice to the victims. There has been a purging in society at many levels and new regulations brought in to try and ensure good governance. I believe that this will bring a new level of justice in society. One of the most profound human senses is the sense of injustice which brings with it the sense of oppression and helplessness. Jesus came to set the oppressed free, and this focus on justice issues has come to the fore increasingly in Christian mission as integral to the Gospel.

Different Levels of Spiritual Authority

We live in the era where we have different levels of territory superimposed on one another. For example, in the natural world, I own a house with a substantial garden. I hold the title deeds and have sole authority to occupy that house and grounds, with my wife. But there is a blackbird that has included my garden as part of his territory and if another blackbird comes he chases it out of his boundaries. And there is a robin who is particularly insistent on not allowing any other robin share his territory in my garden. My boundaries do not correspond with the robin's boundaries or the local fox that has a considerably larger territory!

Similarly, in the spiritual realm, there are both superimposed and overlapping territories in the same parcel of earth. There are national governments and local authorities which have legitimate spheres of authority either of which may open spiritual doors to good or evil spiritual powers. There may be local witches' covens or Freemasons who have taken territory where they exercise a malign influence and give legal rights to the enemy.

Then there is the church which has been given the mandate by Jesus to spread the Kingdom of God over all the earth and thus release the angelic powers to exercise their full function on God's behalf, binding and banishing the powers of darkness from their spheres of control. This leads to a clash of the kingdoms as differing spiritual authorities and powers vie for control in any given territory. It is of crucial importance that we understand what part of this mandate is ours and what part belongs to the angels. We cannot do their part and they will not do our part.

We see this distinction clearly in Daniel 10.
*"In the third year of Cyrus king of Persia, **a revelation was given to Daniel** [who was called Belteshazzar]. Its message was true and it concerned a **great war**. The **understanding** of the message came to him in a **vision**.*

At that time I, Daniel, mourned for three weeks. I ate no choice food; no meat or wine touched my lips; and I used no lotions at all until the three weeks were over.

On the twenty-fourth day of the first month, as I was standing on the bank of the great river, the Tigris, I looked up and there before me was a man dressed in linen, *with a belt of fine gold from Uphaz around his waist. His body was like topaz, his face like lightning, his eyes like flaming torches, his arms and legs like the gleam of burnished bronze, and his voice like the sound of a multitude.*

*I, Daniel, was the only one who saw the vision; those who were with me did not see it, but such terror overwhelmed them that they fled and hid themselves. So I was left alone, gazing at this great vision; I had no strength left, my face turned deathly pale and **I was helpless**. Then I heard him speaking, and as I listened to him, I fell into a **deep sleep, my face to the ground.***

*A hand touched me and set me trembling on my hands and knees. He said, 'Daniel, you who are highly esteemed, **consider carefully the words I am about to speak to you**, and stand up, for I have now been sent to you.' And when he said this to me, I stood up trembling.*

*Then he continued, 'Do not be afraid, Daniel. **Since the first day that you set your mind to gain understanding and to humble yourself before your God, your words were heard, and I have come in response to them.** <u>But the prince of the Persian kingdom resisted me twenty-one days</u>. **Then Michael, one of the chief princes, came to help me**, because I was detained there with the king of Persia.*

***Now I have come to explain to you** what will happen to your people in the future, for the vision concerns a time yet to come.'*

While he was saying this to me, I bowed with my face toward the ground and was speechless. Then one who looked like a man touched my lips, and I opened my mouth and began to speak. I said to the one standing before me, 'I am overcome with anguish because of the vision, my lord, and I feel very weak. How can I, your servant, talk with you, my lord? My strength is gone and I can hardly breathe.'

Again the one who looked like a man touched me and gave me strength. 'Do not be afraid, you who are highly esteemed,' he said. 'Peace! Be strong now; be strong.'

When he spoke to me, I was strengthened and said, 'Speak, my lord, since you have given me strength.'

So he said, 'Do you know why I have come to you? **Soon I will return to fight against the prince of Persia, and when I go, the prince of Greece will come;** *but first I will tell you what is written in the Book of Truth.* **No one supports me against them except Michael, your prince.***"*

Territorial Powers in Conflict

Daniel was a highly placed government minister in the Persian Empire, one of 3 ministers who oversaw the 120 regions of the empire. [Daniel 6:1-2]. But he was also a Jew, having been taken captive as a youth of about 16 by Nebuchadnezzar, King of the Babylonian Empire, which preceded the Persian Empire. He had remained faithful to God throughout despite much opposition and many trials. He was clearly positioned by God in this high office in a pagan regime where sorcerers, enchanters, mediums and astrologers were the main sources of spiritual guidance and direction. [Daniel 2:2]. He was not overwhelmed by the spiritual darkness which surrounded him but remained someone who operated in the heavenly realms of light, revelation, vision and dream as God's light in a dark place. During the days of the Babylonian Empire he had been made ruler over the province of Babylon and in charge of all its wise men - the sorcerers, enchanters, magicians and astrologers!! [Daniel 2:48].

His light shone brighter than their combined darkness.

Spiritual Principalities

The spiritual principality or territorial spirit reigning over Persia, described as the "prince of Persia" was on the dark side and was empowered or given authority by the Emperor as the legitimate ruler. The Emperor by his worship of other gods gave legitimacy to this dark prince. This prince of darkness clearly opposed Daniel and God's purposes and resisted strongly the revelation which was being given to Daniel and blocked off its understanding for 21 days. The overall theme of Daniel's various revelations was about territorial warfare which would significantly affect Israel and the surrounding nations and would ultimately result in the consummation of God's kingdom on earth.

"Then the sovereignty, power and greatness of all the kingdoms under heaven will be handed over to the holy people of the Most High. His kingdom will be an everlasting kingdom, and all rulers will worship and obey him." Daniel 7:27

The prince of Persia wanted to block this revelation of God's territorial purposes and resisted the angel bringing the revelation to Daniel. The revealing angel was obviously of lower rank than the territorial prince and was not succeeding on his own. But Daniel, as a Jew, in loyal submission to God and His purposes for his people had a level of authority in the spirit realm even in a pagan jurisdiction. So he gives himself to prayer and fasting specifically for revelation.

After 3 weeks the angel bringing revelation appeared to Daniel in human form, but not like a normal man. He was an awesome being with a voice like the sound of a multitude. The men with Daniel didn't see him but were overwhelmed with dread and fled while Daniel fell to the ground in a deep sleep. Then the angel touched him and set him trembling on his hands and knees. The vision was so overwhelming that Daniel's breath and strength were taken away. He could hardly breathe or stand up. Then the angel strengthened him and told Daniel to consider carefully what he was about to tell him. So Daniel stood up and listened intently to the revelation.

This revelation is of vital importance to us too, for an understanding of our role, as opposed to the angels' roles in spiritual warfare:

- Daniel was highly esteemed by God. The man of God, or intercessor, man or woman, who seeks God for revelation of God's purposes, is highly ranked on God's value system and is positioned to receive from God.

- Setting one's mind with determination to gain understanding through humbling oneself in prayer and fasting gains heaven's ear immediately, even if the response is delayed in getting back to earth.

- An angel was dispatched in response to Daniel's prayer. We can expect angels to be activated as we pray to God, especially as we pray from revelation, and for revelation. Angels spring into action as we pray prayers of declaration in response to revelation.

- There may be spiritual opposition in the heavenly places - not to our prayers getting through - but to the answers getting back to us. With satan's angels opposing God's angels - they may delay the answer but not stop it if we persevere in prayer.

- Our priority is to keep engaged with God in prayer, worship, declaration, fasting, rather than engaging the enemy other than resisting him when he attacks us.

- God will send angelic reinforcements when necessary. He sent Michael, the prince of Daniel's people, to support the angel bringing the revelation.

- It was primarily the role of the angels to engage the dark principalities not Daniel's. *[There are those who say that we can engage principalities and I know of some mature ministries who have done so because they felt that God led them to do so. But I do not find any biblical example of this. At least it would need to be proven ministries of governmental rank, who had received a clear mandate from God to do so. Christians who step beyond their spiritual authority risk a serious backlash.]* The revelatory angel was going to engage in further spiritual warfare after leaving Daniel, engaging again the prince of Persia and then the prince of Greece.

• The angel strengthened Daniel and proceeded to reveal to him what was written in the *"Book of Truth"* [chapter 11].

• Then 2 more angels appeared to Daniel [12:5] and the final revelation he was given concerned his own allotted inheritance. *"As for you, go your way till the end. You will **rest**, and then at the end of the days you will **rise to receive your allotted inheritance.**"* Daniel 12:13

Whatever territory God has assigned to us in this life, our faithfulness in pursuing it and laying hold of it, has a bearing on the inheritance we will receive in the life to come. We do not receive our final territorial inheritance here in this age. We will rest for a season after our earthly labours, then, at the resurrection we will receive our final inheritance. In the parable of the minas [or talents] Jesus showed that our inheritance will comprise a sphere of jurisdiction [over 5 cities, or 10 cities etc] corresponding to our level of faithfulness in what was entrusted to us in this life.

Daniel brought in the reign of God to many situations in the hostile environment where God had placed him. He excelled in the realm of revelation, dreams, visions, understanding, interpretation and wisdom to manifest the kingdom of God to be superior to all the counterfeit revelations of the enemy's domain. He took that territory and thereby brought the mighty pagan Babylonian Emperor Nebuchadnezzar to glorify God.

"Now I, Nebuchadnezzar, praise and exalt and glorify the King of heaven, because everything he does is right and all his ways are just. And those who walk in pride he is able to humble." Daniel 4:34

What a kingdom triumph for this faithful man of God! And angels were on hand to help him take his territory.

"Abraham's blessing and destiny was attached to the territory God had assigned to him."

CHAPTER 7

Our Assigned Sphere or Territory

God has assigned territories to all of His children. In the superimposed and overlapping territories that there are in life, there is a particular sphere which he has assigned to each of us. The apostle Paul knew his sphere.

"We, however, will not boast beyond proper limits, but will confine our boasting to the sphere of service God himself has assigned to us, a sphere that also includes you." 2 Corinthians 10:13

As the apostle to the Gentiles, Paul was assigned his specific sphere in terms of people group, the non - Jewish peoples, although he made a point of preaching to the Jews first wherever he went. In terms of geographical territory he went in ever increasing circles from Antioch, especially where the Gospel had not yet been preached. He was guided by the leading of the Holy Spirit as to the timing of his ministry in any specific part of that territory. For instance, in Acts 16:6 he was *"kept by the Holy Spirit from preaching the word in the province of Asia"*. It was God's timing for Macedonia as he realised through the vision he received at Troas, of a man of Macedonia begging, *"Come over to Macedonia and help us"*. Acts 16:9-10.

Later he would preach in Asia and would make Ephesus the centre of his ministry for that season and this season was so effective that *"all the Jews and Greeks who lived in the province of Asia heard the word of the Lord".* Acts 19:10. So for Paul, the people group, the geographical territory and the timing were all important.

Angelic Encouragement

The last assignment of Paul's that we read about in Acts was the assignment to go to Rome. The one occasion when Paul saw the angel assigned to him for this trip was when in danger during the shipwrecked journey across the Mediterranean. He tells the soldiers and sailors and whole company on the ship about this.

*"Men, you should have taken my advice not to sail from Crete; then you would have spared yourselves this damage and loss. But now I urge you to keep up your courage, because not one of you will be lost; only the ship will be destroyed. Last night **an angel** of the God to whom I belong and whom I serve stood beside me and said, 'Do not be afraid, Paul. You must stand trial before Caesar; and God has graciously given you the lives of all who sail with you.' So keep up your courage, men, for I have faith in God that it will happen just as he told me. Nevertheless, we must run aground on some island."* Acts 27:21-26

Paul reports this angelic visitation in a matter of fact way, as if it was nothing unusual for him. He was used to visions and revelations. In 2 Corinthians 12:7 he says that he was also given a messenger [*angel*] of satan to harass him to keep him from getting conceited because of the abundance of revelations he had received.

Earlier, in Acts 23:11, when Paul was arrested in Jerusalem after an uproar among the people God spoke to Paul about this assignment.

"The following night the Lord stood near Paul and said, Take courage! As you have testified about me in Jerusalem, so you must also testify in Rome."

Not only were very clear words spoken to Paul by the Lord but the Lord actually stood near Paul. This could have been a vision of the

Lord as on the road to Damascus or it could possibly have been the angel of the Lord, an angel who mediated God's presence as happened so often in the Old Testament. This happened at a crucial time for Paul's personal safety as 40 Jews had bound themselves with an oath not to eat or drink till they had killed Paul. There was a real clash of the kingdoms with satan's human agents hell-bent on murder and using fasting to access demonic aid to their cause. But God's purpose was that Paul *"must also testify in Rome"*.

Demonic Harassment

God gave him the strongest possible indication of this next assignment by speaking to him personally, by Jesus standing beside him and speaking to him either in person or via an angel. This no doubt prompted Paul to appeal to Caesar, which in turn led to his sea voyage to Rome in which he was shipwrecked. Here again I think it is fairly safe to assume that in the storm were demonic forces trying to prevent Paul's assignment succeeding. This may well have been another episode where the angel of satan was harassing him. He gives quite a list of these harassments in 2 Corinthians 11:23-27

"I have worked much harder, been in prison more frequently, been flogged more severely, and been exposed to death again and again. Five times I received from the Jews the forty lashes minus one. Three times I was beaten with rods, once I was pelted with stones, three times I was shipwrecked, I spent a night and a day in the open sea, I have been constantly on the move. I have been in danger from rivers, in danger from bandits, in danger from my fellow Jews, in danger from Gentiles; in danger in the city, in danger in the country, in danger at sea; and in danger from false believers. I have laboured and toiled and have often gone without sleep; I have known hunger and thirst and have often gone without food; I have been cold and naked."

When Jesus faced a similar unnatural storm on the Sea of Galilee he rebuked the wind and the waves saying, *"Be muzzled!"* It seems that he was rebuking the demonic powers stirring up the wind and waves, because there was an instant calm after Jesus authoritative command. In a normal storm it takes time for the sea to settle down again. Jesus had an important assignment on the other side of the Sea to deliver the Gadarene man Legion, so terribly oppressed by satan's legion of demons. The evil one obviously didn't want that to happen and sought to sabotage Jesus' assignment.

In the case of Paul's shipwreck God sent His angel to speak to Paul in the height of the crisis to assure him of the success of his mission and that God had given him the lives of those with him as well, and also some territory on the island of Malta. Paul was committed to take all the territory God had assigned to him and all God's resources were there to assist in the mission. Angels are a vital part of that, although it is not often that they are seen. In their essential essence they are invisible spirit beings operating in the spirit realm unobserved by our eyes. But in this particular case Paul was aware that an angel of the Lord stood beside him and spoke a clear message of encouragement to him.

Cessasionist Objections

Unfortunately many today, and indeed through Christian history, have no place in their thinking or experience for the active working of angels, or are suspicious of any angelic appearances. Luther said *"May God not send me visions or angels, I wouldn't know how to handle it"*. [Quoted by Ami Bost 'Les prophètes protestants', Melun 1847, pp III, IV]. Indeed when angelic manifestations were plentiful, singing in the skies night after night, during the time of the Huguenot revival, there was a whole section of the Calvinistic Protestants who considered the reports spurious. The Cartesian rationalism of the Renaissance age had so penetrated the church that they had difficulty coping with the supernatural. That continues to be the case for many who have taken a Cessasionist viewpoint on anything supernatural today.

When I was a student at university, a visiting speaker was asked to give a talk on *"Miracles"*. He gave a very thorough presentation on why the miracles recorded in the Bible were authentic and should be believed. During the question time afterwards one student asked him if miracles could happen today. He clearly did not believe so, but could give no solid biblical reason for rejecting the possibility, especially given the forceful argument he had just given to defend the genuineness of the biblical miracles. He was totally at a loss to explain the miracles people gave testimony about.

However, Evangelical Christians, who by definition, are committed to the unchanging nature of God and His Word, must engage faithfully with every aspect of truth, teaching and manifestation of the angelic that we see in Scripture, and expect the same in our day and age.

An Assignment in Ireland

Angels had not been to the fore in my thinking or experience till in recent years. However in retrospect, I have to acknowledge that they have been at work, even if I haven't always been aware of their activity. When God first assigned me to a territory in the West of Ireland, I was aware of operating in a very different "spiritual atmosphere"than that to which I had been accustomed in the North of Ireland. Each time we crossed the border into the Republic we were aware that we were entering a different *"principality"*. It seemed more *"oppressive"*and spiritually *"dark"* and I gradually became more and more depressed, though that had never been my disposition previously. I felt like I was wading through spiritual treacle rather than flowing in the fullness of God. Even within the Republic of Ireland there seemed to be different territories roughly corresponding to the historic provinces.

I remember on one occasion in 1987, when we had been to a Fire Conference hosted in Frankfurt by Reinhart Bonnke, we had been so impacted by the spiritual atmosphere of that conference that we decided to pray all the way from Dublin in the east to Galway in the west, as we drove home. But as soon as we crossed the river Shannon in Athlone and entered the province of Connacht, I sensed we had entered a different spiritual territory and we were back to the heaviness of the region we had been working in for the previous 7 years.

But I felt God gave us the assignment to do something about it. A few years previously I had seen a vision of a lighted match come to the map of the west of Ireland. It ignited the map at Loop head in County Clare and then burned a trail all the way north to Galway city, where it became a furnace. Then the flame went west around the coast and eventually encircled the province of Connacht. I hadn't known what to do with the vision at the time, but took great encouragement from it that God was somehow going to ignite a spiritual fire in our territory in the West of Ireland.

Then, at this conference in Frankfurt, the Lord spoke to me one day at 1pm while I was outside the conference venue during the lunch break. He told me to go back and take some men and *"prayer- walk"* the route I had seen that flame taking in that vision 5 years previously. I called the little church together in our home when we got back and shared this with them, and 4 men decided to do the first stage of that prayer walk. We continued to cover the territory, section by section over the next 24 years until we had encircled that whole province in prayer and the spiritual atmosphere had changed. Gradually a network of churches spread around a territory that had very few evangelical believers when I first visited it in 1970. Things gradually changed to the point where I no longer noticed the same oppressiveness in the spiritual atmosphere.

Initially I didn't fully realise that angels were involved in shifting atmospheres and that the strategy God had given me was in many ways similar to that given to Abraham to walk around the length and breadth of his assigned territory raising prayer altars to the Lord.

Adam's Territory

Adam had been given 2 assignments in relation to territory. The first one was in relation to the garden of Eden.
"The LORD God took the man and put him in the garden of Eden to work it and keep it." Genesis 2:15 [ESV]

Adam had been given this territory to guard and cultivate - a little piece of the kingdom of heaven on earth - a garden paradise in Eden. It was God's model of what the whole earth was to look like if Adam had fulfilled his dual mandate. But Adam would have to guard his territory and keep the devil out of it by the authority God had given him over everything that moved on the face of the earth. Instead he entertained the devil who deceitfully had slithered in and had not been discerned for what he really was by Adam. He was the usurper who tricked Adam into giving him the legal right to the garden through Adam's disobedience to God. Hence Adam lost his territory and was put out of the garden by God. It now belonged legally to satan because man had surrendered it to him.

Adam's second territorial mandate had been to extend the domain of the earthly Paradise to embrace the whole earth.

"Then God said, 'Let us make mankind in our image, in our likeness, so that they may rule over the fish in the sea and the birds in the sky, over the livestock and all the wild animals, and over all the creatures that move along the ground.'

So God created mankind in his own image, in the image of God he created them;

male and female he created them. God blessed them and said to them, 'Be fruitful and increase in number; fill the earth and subdue it. Rule over the fish in the sea and the birds in the sky and over every living creature that moves on the ground.'" Genesis 1:26-28

Adam and his offspring were to gradually extend the garden paradise God had given him till it extended over the face of the whole earth. *"Be fruitful and increase in number; fill the earth and subdue it."* That was God's original plan for the planet and his strategy to achieve it was through man bringing in the kingdom of God to the earth realm. That remains God's plan today. However, Adam failed to guard the garden and lost what he had, so was no longer able to fulfil the second part of his territorial mandate. But God's plan remained, and was to be picked up by Abraham, in the next phase of its outworking!

Abraham's Territory

Abraham wasn't given a paradise to start with. He was brought up in a pagan moon-worshipping, but affluent nation in what is still known as the cradle of civilisation. When he was but one man God called him with a view to blessing him and making him abundantly fruitful so that he could pick up on God's plan, beginning with a new patch of terra ferma where God would establish, through Abraham, an outpost of heaven on earth and from there bless the world and advance his kingdom on earth.

"The LORD had said to Abram, Go from your country, your people and your father's household to the land I will show you. I will make you into a great nation, and I will bless you; I will make your name great, and you will be a blessing. I will bless those who bless you, and whoever curses you I will curse; and all peoples on earth will be blessed through you."
Genesis 12:1-3

God had a land, a territory in view for Abraham. Taking territory is important in God's plan. Abraham would have to leave the land he was in and any hopes of inheriting land there in that it was not God's territory for him. He would have to believe God's word, trust God and obey, without knowing exactly where this territory was. Abraham's blessing and destiny was attached to the territory God had assigned to him. Abraham obeyed and set out dependant daily on

God's directions, till he arrived at a place where God said to him, *"To your offspring I will give* **this land** *so he built an altar* **there** *to the Lord."* Genesis 12:7.

Abraham's Strategy for Taking His Territory

God showed him his assigned territory and he dedicated it to the Lord by building an altar there to the Lord. He still didn't know the full extent of his territory so he journeyed around exploring it and building altars to the Lord. *"From there he went on toward the hills east of Bethel and pitched his tent, with Bethel on the west and Ai on the east. There he built an altar to the LORD and called on the name of the LORD."* Genesis 12:8

Abraham's focus was not on building a house for himself but on building an altar to the Lord. A tent would do for himself. Archaeology has shown us that in Ur, where Abraham had come from, there were well-developed houses and presumably Abraham had been used to living in a house not a tent. He would keep building altars to the Lord because the territory was to be God's permanently. He would not settle in a permanent residence himself but keep on the move exploring the extent of the territory God had for him.

Eventually God said to him after Lot had parted from him:
"Look around from where you are, to the north and south, to the east and west. **All the land that you see** *I will give to you and your offspring forever. I will make your offspring like the dust of the earth, so that if anyone could count the dust, then your offspring could be counted.* **Go, walk through the length and breadth of the land, for I am giving it to you.** *So Abram went to live near the great trees of Mamre at Hebron, where he pitched his tents. There he* **built an altar** *to the LORD."* Genesis 13:14-18 [NIVUK]

This time God specifies to him that his territory will be the extent of his vision. He was told to look around in every direction and fill his vision with the land. Then he was told to walk throughout the length and breadth of the land as part of taking it. God later told Joshua, *"every place that the sole of your foot will tread I have given it to you"*. Joshua 1:3

God's instruction to us for Galway and Connacht was quite similar. We were to walk and pray around the circumference of individual towns we were reaching out to and around the circumference of the entire territory. There is something very real and earthy about praying while walking in the actual territory, and for the people one sees. It was a tremendous experience for those who joined with us on different occasions.

On one occasion, when we stopped for lunch we felt to break bread together and share communion. We felt that, as a prophetic act, we should pour out the remainder of the bottle of wine on the earth to declare that the blood of Christ was shed for the people of that territory. When we did so, one of the men had a vision of a shepherd going to fetch one sheep from one hill, one from another hill and one from a different hill and bringing them together in a little flock on the strand by the sea. At the time there were no evangelical churches of any description for many miles in any direction from that coastal spot. But we felt that we should pray for God to send someone with a pastoral call and gift to that area. We continued to pray that prayer from time to time for the next couple of years. We felt restrained from doing the next section of the prayer walk till God moved us again, because we sensed that God needed to move pieces or people into position before we could move on.

Two years later we got the green light from God to prayer walk the next section of coast - about 50 miles. And this time we were led to do a month of evangelism in that area as well. We organised a programme of outreach which included going out into the streets to talk to people about the Lord. We also hired a local hotel room to hold individual prayer sessions with people who wanted prayer for healing. We went on local radio to invite people along and we did evening evangelistic meetings in the hotel.

On one Saturday when all these things were planned and we had a team of about 40 people who had travelled from other parts to help, there was a terrible storm. The rain was pouring down and the wind was howling when we met in the hotel to pray and the weather forecast for the day was for that to continue. Not very good for talking to people on the streets because they wouldn't be out in that kind of weather! So when we met together to pray as a team in the morning I felt the Holy Spirit came on me to call the weather into line with God's purposes for that day. We had a powerful time of prayer and the rain cleared up. We had a great day with many opportunities to share the Gospel and pray for the sick and for people to come to the Lord. Late that night I happened to see the late night weather forecast and was amazed to hear the weather forecaster refer to the fact that they had got the weather wrong for that day and had no explanation for it! I suspect some territorial angels were at work to help us begin to take that territory for the Lord.

One of the men who had received prayer the previous Saturday wanted to come back that Saturday to tell us about his healing, as we had suggested. But he had no car and lived 12 miles away. When he got up in the morning and saw the rain, he thought he would not be able to make it to town. Then suddenly the rain cleared and he was able to come in and share how God had healed him when we had prayed for him.

Amazingly, at the end of that outreach, a man and his wife came to me and said that they felt God was calling them to leave their home in the North of Ireland and move to that area to take care of the folks who had just come to the Lord. They travelled initially every week to do an Alpha course with the new believers. This involved a 4 hour trip each way often arriving home at 3am, and they did this for 6 months or so while they looked for a house. They were having great difficulty finding something until one weekend they packed the car and said they would not come back till they got something. Then God provided. They have been there for many years now and there is a significant shift in the spiritual atmosphere as they have made their home a house of prayer where people come to receive God's love through them. People have been healed of cancer and depression and come to know the Lord.

We have often found that there is a spiritual battle over new territory. The powers in the atmosphere for a long time don't want to give way. But if we persist in obedience to God with perseverance and faith then the angels God has assigned to the territory come to our aid. They are there to *"search out a place for us to camp"* as they were for Israel.

As Abraham walked through his assigned territory he established a presence of God in the land as he raised up the altars of prayer, praise and worship to God. Later he was aware of angels being with him and helping him in his territorial assignment. On one particular occasion he had a visit from 3 angels.

In Genesis 18, Abraham had 3 angelic visitors in human form. This passage is introduced by saying that *"The Lord appeared to Abraham"* [v1]. It would appear that this was a theophany, some have suggested a triune theophany, but it later appears that at least 2 of the 3 who appeared as men, were angels. [Genesis 19:1]. Abraham prepared a meal for his 3 celestial visitors and it was in this encounter that the Lord specifically promised that his wife Sarah would have a son in a year's time. [v10]. This was a critical phase in the fulfilment of the territorial promise to Abraham and his descendants. He had already been waiting and believing for 24 years for this promise to be fulfilled. Now God shows up personally with 2 angels in human form with a specific promise to Sarah that she would bear the son who would inherit the land. Hagar's son by Abraham would not inherit it.

Forty years later, when Abraham sent his servant to Haran to find a wife for Isaac he specifically commanded him not to take his son back to that land because his inheritance was in Canaan.

"The servant asked him, 'What if the woman is unwilling to come back with me to this land? Shall I then take your son back to the country you came from?'

'Make sure that you do not take my son back there,' Abraham said. 'The LORD, the God of heaven, who brought me out of my father's household and my native land and who spoke to me and promised me on oath, saying,

'To your offspring I will give this land'— ***he will send his angel before you*** *so that you can get a wife for my son from there. If the woman is unwilling to come back with you, then you will be released from this oath of mine. Only do not take my son back there."* Genesis 24:5-7

This was a crucial event which would prepare for the passing of the baton to the next generation to take the assigned territory. Often a relay race is lost in the passing of the baton. But Abraham knew that God was on the case and that he would send his angel to ensure the success of the mission. As one reads the amazing way that romantic story unfolded one can have no doubt that the angel did a good job. Isaac had to stay in the assigned territory and God would send an angel to bring a wife to ensure that took place.

God and the two angels who visited Abraham with him shared with Abraham the situation about the wickedness of Sodom and his plans to destroy it. This stirred Abraham to intercession knowing that his nephew Lot lived there. While his intercession did not spare Sodom the angels rescued Lot and saved him and his daughters from sharing in their fate. So Abraham, in praying throughout the land and in raising up altars to the Lord, seems to have established an angelic presence in the land. These territorial angels were activated through Abraham's spiritual activity and helped him in his assignment. But Abraham did not drive out the Canaanites or demolish their altars to false gods which had given the dark angels space to operate. He assignment was positive not negative. One does not have to drive out the darkness. One has just to shine the light. Daniel did not engage with the dark prince who held sway over the empire in which he lived, but engaged with God in prayer, and God sent a stronger angelic prince to deal with the prince of darkness.

There is an interesting chapter, "Binding the Strong Man" in Norman Grubb's book, *"Rees Howells Intercessor"* [Lutterworth Press, London. 1973]. Rees Howells says that he became increasingly conscious of the Holy Spirit engaging the enemy in battle and overcoming him, until he would be finally assured of victory. He could see the Holy Spirit binding the strong man as he maintained his place in intercession. The Spirit would then tell him that the intercession was finished and the position gained. He would then await visible deliverance in praise and faith.

Psalm 149 teaches us that the high praises of God in our mouths are like a double-edged sword in our hands to bind kings with shackles and carry out the sentence God has decreed against them. Our praise effects God's decrees against the enemy and binds the strong man so that his house can be plundered. As Abraham raised up his altars of prayer around Canaan he laid a foundation for his descendants who would later drive out the Canaanites and take possession of their territory.

Owning Property in Our Territory

In 1991 we purchased a site for the construction of our first church premises in Galway city. We discovered that in actually owning a piece of terra ferma we were taking a further step in taking the territory for the Lord. This step was a real step of faith which met significant opposition in various ways. The Republic of Ireland was, at that stage, intolerant of anything other than the dominant religion. Since the foundation of the Irish State in 1921 the population of Evangelical Christians had steadily dwindled through emigration, persecution and discrimination. The Protestant churches were gradually closing or had very small congregations especially in the West, and new evangelical church buildings were virtually unheard of.

When we applied for planning permission we knew we would be up against a lot of prejudice. People had already protested with banners outside our rented Christian bookshop denouncing us as a brainwashing cult. Some of the first believers had lost their jobs, were unable to get a job, or were disinherited by their parents just because of their new found faith in Christ. So, in this prevailing atmosphere we covered the planning application in prayer in our 6am prayer meetings. Indeed God specifically told us to do so.

It was only after we received the planning permission that we discovered the lengths God had gone to in order to answer our prayers. It emerged that a new young engineer was moved into the planning office and our application was one of the first to arrive on his desk. He consulted with the senior engineer who said *"Oh we can't let that lot get planning!"* His comments were a reflection of the prevailing prejudice and not based on proper planning criteria. However, the junior engineer who had to deal with the application dealt with it on engineering criteria, made one condition which was necessary for building regulations and passed the application. He was moved out of that office after only 3 weeks!

It was through that application that he heard about us and was curious to find out more because God had appeared to him in a vision shortly before that and he was open. He immediately gave his life to the Lord and started to attend our church. When our building was eventually constructed he ended up living in the apartment upstairs!

I felt that we should invite the mayor of the city to officiate at the opening ceremony. Most of our folks had such an underground mentality up to that point that they didn't think that the mayor would come. But I felt, a little bit like Paul in Philippi insisting that the Roman officers come publicly and release him rather than let him out the back door. I felt it was time to take a public profile after our years of *"hiddeness"* in homes. The mayor accepted. Just before the opening ceremony he asked me how we had managed to get planning permission. He was obviously well aware of the prejudice. Later on he asked again *"Are you sure you got planning permission?"* He was absolutely astounded.

When we bought the site initially we walked around it to pray and dedicate it to the Lord and stake it our as our territory. However during the building works we had a lot of problems with vandalism. There was one attempt to burn the building down but the fire got put out before it really took hold. So we had to pray specifically for protection and security. We prayed till we felt we had broken through and got our response and someone saw a picture of angels being stationed on the roof of the building to watch over it. From then on the vandalism ceased. Praise God for angels who station themselves on the territory God has assigned to us.

In later years we became aware of witches' curses that had been uttered against us, recorded on cassette tape and strung across our entrance. We found that it was necessary repeatedly to reaffirm our dedication of the territory to the Lord by praying around it to cleanse it and keep it holy for God. Likewise when we purchased our own home for the first time we walked the territory to dedicate the ground inside and outside to the Lord.

Our house was built in a new development on a relatively high place overlooking the city. There was a blackthorn *"spirit bush"* at the top of the hill behind our house. We were told that none of the builders would touch it or remove it because of superstitious fear of *"bad luck"*. They felt it had power. So we likewise felt that we should dedicate, not just our house, but pray around the estate and establish the presence of God in the place knowing that he is much greater than any other spirit. Also in the city we changed our approach to handling negative things which we felt were opening the door to dark powers. At one stage, when there was a public parade of witches through the city, we thought we should protest with placards. But we later realised we were using human methods that were ineffective spiritually and were probably antagonising people rather than achieving anything for the kingdom of God. At a later stage the local performing groups used the arts to open spiritual doors through conjuring up things from the pagan past and parading dragons and mythical creatures through the city in a public attempt to activate pagan and Druidic powers. Rather than protest, at this stage, we felt we should follow the event a few days later by prayer-walking the parade route in reverse, to close any spiritual doors that had been opened and lift up the name of Jesus through worship of the one true God who is far above all principalities and powers and every name that can be named both in heaven and earth and under the earth.

Abraham had gone throughout his territory building altars to the Lord. In Romans 4:13 Paul interprets all the promises God had given to Abraham and his offspring to mean that they would inherit the entire world.

*"It was not through the law that Abraham and his offspring received the promise that he would be heir **of the world**, but through the righteousness that comes by faith."*

This would take place through his spiritual offspring from all the nations of the world who through faith in Christ are made righteous. While his natural offspring were promised the land of Israel, his spiritual sons were promised the whole earth. So we follow in the footsteps of our father Abraham when we go through the territory where we live, that God has assigned to us and raise altars of worship and intercession to God, and when we by faith lay hold of the promises God has given to us for our specifically assigned territory.

Other, Non-Geographical Territories

Sometimes the territory God has assigned to us is not so much geographical. It may be to deal with a certain issue or section of society that needs a spiritual breakthrough to release people from bondage, oppression or addiction. Some people are specifically assigned to work with drug addicts, alcoholics, the homeless or some other grouping for which God gives them an assignment and a "sphere" of ministry.

After we had spent 20 years planting and establishing the church in Galway on the west coast of Ireland, we felt that God was moving us on to be more centrally located for the nation. For a while we didn't know exactly where to go. Then one morning God spoke separately to me and my wife and told us to go to the Roscommon side of Athlone. When we found a particular property in that location we knew it was where God wanted us to be. I believe that where we live is important. But we did not know the full scope of what God wanted us to do there.

Shortly afterwards I was at a prayer day in another part of the country. As an aid to prayer, someone had taken newspaper clippings of various problems or issues around the country and pasted them on the walls of the prayer room. One of those immediately caught my attention. It headlined, *"9 Suicides in 9 weeks in Roscommon!"* Having just moved to Roscommon, which is a small rural town and county with a small population, I was shocked by the statistic and began to pray about that issue. One day I was praying in a local wood near our home as I often did. It was a quiet secluded place and I like to pray while walking around and talking to the Lord. I was on my usual path around the wood when all of a sudden I stopped as I became aware of an intense presence of the Lord. It felt as if I had just stepped into the spirit realm and was aware of a scene taking place in heaven. I could sense or hear the cries of desperate people arising to God's ears. They were the cries of people who had lost hope, who didn't know where to turn and were feeling suicidal. They were not uttered as prayers as such but they were reaching God's ears as prayers. Then the scene changed and I recalled God's words to Moses, *"**I have indeed seen the misery of my people** in Egypt. I have heard them crying out because of their slave drivers, and I am concerned about their suffering.*

*...And now the cry of the Israelites has reached me, and I have seen the way the Egyptians are oppressing them. So now, go. **I am sending you** to Pharaoh to bring my people the Israelites out of Egypt."* [Exodus 3:7-10].

In that moment it felt as if I were standing on holy ground in the presence of angels, not a burning bush as Moses was, and that God was giving me a new assignment, a new sphere of ministry alongside some of the other things we were already doing. Like Moses, I felt completely inadequate for that and was cast totally on the Lord. But we saw God intervene dramatically to rescue people who were suicidal and give them a life worth living. We produced educational DVDS for schools and RTE, our national TV broadcaster contacted us and filmed our programme being presented in a school and showed it on prime time television. While this was by no means our primary activity at this stage, because it was addressing an issue that had come to national attention as a major issue in Irish society at that time, it gave us a profile on the national stage which we would not otherwise have had.

Ironically, the traditional churches which had been so antagonistic to us 20 years previously, now began to ask us to train some of their priests in handling suicidal issues. And the Catholic bishops of

Ireland, England, Scotland and Wales asked me to draft a document about suicide, which would be distributed at Mass in all 4 countries! I felt that God had given me a particular strategy which was quite different to, although complementary to the secular programmes, which by their nature did not address the significant spiritual issues underlying suicide. If God wants us to take territory for the kingdom of God then the church has to have God's kingdom answers for the societal issues that confound the wisdom of this world. It's thrilling to see someone who was once on the way to end their life, now happily serving God and living a fulfilled life. I believe God has an assigned territory for each one of us and it may change at different seasons of life. For some it may be to impact a nation or town or geographical region significantly for the Lord. For others it may be their street, their neighbours, their work colleagues, their school or college, their business, their family or friends. For others it may be in addressing some local issue or societal problem with kingdom values and answers.

I think of the work of movements like Teen Challenge who have addressed the drug issues or the International Justice Mission who are using the skills of the legal profession dedicated to bringing justice to areas of abuse and corruption like people trafficking. Each of us has a sphere and God has assigned His angelic helpers to come to our aid in doing the impossible, no matter what God has assigned to us.

"So as Abraham was building altars around the promised land, he was activating angels to act on God's behalf in the territory where they were assigned."

CHAPTER 8

Angels and Intercession

A number of years ago the Lord dropped into my spirit a biblical reference - Exodus 30:6. God has often guided me through Scripture but this was the first time He had done so by just giving me a biblical reference. I didn't know what the verse was about without looking it up. When I did so I discovered that it was about the positioning of the altar of incense in the tabernacle.

"Put the altar in front of the curtain that shields the ark of the covenant law—before the atonement cover that is over the tablets of the covenant law—where I will meet with you."

As I meditated on that verse in its context I realised that the positioning of the altar of incense was central to the functioning of the Old Testament priests. It was in the Holy Place just in front of the curtain which separated it from the Most Holy Place with the mercy seat and the Shekinah glory presence of God. It was the nearest that the ordinary priests got to the glory of God. Many of them must have wondered what it would be like if they could be the high priest and go behind that curtain once a year with the atoning blood. But that curtain separated them from the most intimate expression of the presence of God on earth. And that was where they were to exercise their priestly ministry of intercession. They would bring the needs of the people before God who was enthroned between the cherubim above the mercy seat. As they put incense upon the coals taken from the altar of burnt offering, the bronze altar outside the tabernacle, their prayers would ascend before God from that golden altar of incense. Then they would go out to the people to bless them in the name of the Lord. They would go before God on behalf of the people and then go before the people on behalf of God to administer His blessings in His name and put God's name on the people.

I felt God was showing me that this priestly ministry of intercession before God's throne was to be central in our church life and that we were to go out from there to minister to the people who needed God. I felt that I personally needed to reorder my priorities and put prayer and worship first. Secondly I needed to focus on training the believers in God's ways. Then I was to focus on evangelism to proclaim and express the kingdom of God. In order to do so I handed over the pastoral care to the other elders, because I had inadvertently become focussed too much on pastoral care and church administration as our little church had grown. That together with some internal problems had led us to a period of stagnation with no growth for a couple of years. But when I made these changes the church doubled again in the next couple of years as a whole new batch of people came to the Lord.

I must confess though, to my regret, that we did not manage to sustain that central place for the altar of intercession. We would sustain it for a season, then we grew weary or got distracted when other issues displaced it. That is something that God has drawn me back to in a whole new way more recently as being of strategic importance in whatever aspect or territory-taking we are assigned to.

Of course we no longer live in the Old Testament dispensation but the layout of the tabernacle was a copy of the heavenly sanctuary where our priestly ministry takes place. The curtain has been removed by the death of Christ and every Christian is now a king and priest with access directly into the presence of God in heaven through the

Holy Spirit. That is where we come to bring our prayer and worship along with the angels around the throne of God. In Revelation we find that the original golden altar, of which the earthly altar of incense was a copy, is in heaven.

The Golden Altar of Incense in Heaven

"Another angel, who had a golden censer, came and stood at the altar. He was given much incense to offer, with the prayers of all God's people, on the golden altar in front of the throne. The smoke of the incense, together with the prayers of God's people, went up before God from the angel's hand. Then the angel took the censer, filled it with fire from the altar, and hurled it on the earth; and there came peals of thunder, rumblings, flashes of lightning and an earthquake." Revelation 8:3-5

Not only were the prayers of all God's people going up before God from that golden altar, but the angel held the incense which generated the smoke which carried the prayers up before God in a symbolical way. Then the angel took fire from the altar and hurled it to the earth symbolising God's powerful interventions on earth like thunder, rumblings, flashes of lightning and an earthquake. In other words the angels are involved both in offering up our prayers and presenting them before God, and in bringing God's dramatic answers and responses to our prayers.

So as Abraham was building altars around the promised land, he was activating angels to act on God's behalf in the territory where they were assigned. He may not have been aware of the full extent to which this was taking place but he was establishing a powerful expression of God's presence in the land. Isaac, his son continued the practice and eventually settled in Beersheba in the south of the territory.

"Isaac built an altar there and called on the name of the LORD. There he pitched his tent, and there his servants dug a well." Genesis 26:25

It would seem that eventually Isaac felt he had secured the territory and could settle and build a house. Genesis 27:15

Jacob's Revelation of Angels in His Territory

Later when Jacob, Abraham's grandson, was about to flee the land from his brother's anger, God met with him in a way that was totally new to him. He gained a perception of the spiritual realities in the land in a way that he had not realised before.

*"Jacob left Beersheba and set out for Harran. When he reached a certain place, he stopped for the night because the sun had set. Taking one of the stones there, he put it under his head and lay down to sleep. He had a dream in which he saw a stairway resting on the earth, with its top reaching to heaven, **and the angels of God were ascending and descending** on it. There above it stood the LORD, and he said: I am the LORD, the God of your father Abraham and the God of Isaac. I will give you and your descendants the land on which you are lying. Your descendants will be like the dust of the earth, and you will spread out to the west and to the east, to the north and to the south. All peoples on earth will be blessed through you and your offspring.*

I am with you and will watch over you wherever you go, and I will bring you back to this land.

I will not leave you until I have done what I have promised you.

*When Jacob awoke from his sleep, he thought, '**Surely the LORD is in this place, and I was not aware of it.**' He was afraid and said, '**How awesome is this place! This is none other than the house of God; this is the gate of heaven.**'*

Early the next morning Jacob took the stone he had placed under his head and set it up as a pillar and poured oil on top of it. He called that place Bethel, though the city used to be called Luz.

Then Jacob made a vow, saying, If God will be with me and will watch over me on this journey I am taking and will give me food to eat and clothes to wear so that I return safely to my father's household, then the LORD will be my God and this stone that I have set up as a pillar will be God's house, and of all that you give me I will give you a tenth." Genesis 28:10-22

Before he left the promised land Jacob needed to know the extent to which God's presence had already been established in that land through his grandfather's priestly ministry. The significant response of Jacob was, *"Surely the Lord is in this place and I was not aware of it"*. It is possible to be in a territory where God's presence is firmly established and not be aware of it. This experience opened Jacob's self-centred eyes to the greater spiritual realities of which he had not been truly aware. Instead of pursuing God's blessing by cheating his brother for earthly gain he now realised that he needed to look to God as the Source of the blessing and trust in the powerful promise he had just given to him personally.

It was no longer just a case of inheriting the promises God had given to his grandfather and his father. Now God had given those territorial promises to him personally and the presence of angels in the land reinforced the whole experience to him. The angels were not descending and ascending on this ladder between earth and heaven. They were ascending and descending, in that order, because they were now based *"in the land"* while at the same time having access to heaven and were free to move from one to the other. This powerful sense of angels being *"in the land"* was the new revelation God gave me when we first moved to France. And as I studied this concept in Scripture it gave me a further assurance that whenever God gave me a personal assignment of territory and promises to go with it, it included the presence of angels.

The Priority of Prayer Altars in the Land Today

So this reinforced to me yet again that, in my current assignment in France, raising altars of prayer and worship to the Lord are a vital part of the strategy to take the territory and activate the angels who are already assigned to this nation.

Several years ago in Perpignan, after 3 days of prayer and praise, when we concluded there was an amazing electric storm with lightning flashing around the skies for several hours. There was no accompanying rain which would be the normal in our climate, so it seemed to us to be a significant heavenly witness to God's recognition that when we put the altar of incense central in our lives God acts from heaven on our behalf with a heavenly fireworks display. But we are longing for a greater earthly manifestation of God's kingdom through signs and wonders and an outpouring of the Holy Spirit in revival power in this nation again as he did in the past and as he has foretold in the Scriptures, to bring in the final harvest before Jesus returns. May all those inactive territorial angels be reactivated!

Just recently, during a powerful time of breakthrough intercession for our city and region we were meditating on the scene around the throne of God and joining our prayers and praise with that of the angels. As the Spirit fell on us during our declarations a great crescendo of voices arose shouting, *"We crown Jesus!"*. I received a revelation of what was happening in the spirit realms as we were before the throne of God. I could see a strong column of smoke arising from the altar and going straight up into the atmosphere above our city.

Then when it hit a certain level it began to spread out in a horizontal direction like a thin layer of flat cloud spreading over the wider region around the city. Then it seemed that a throne descended from heaven to rest upon the cloud and Someone sat on the throne. He was surrounded by a host of angels. As he would raise his hand to point to a certain place on earth, an angel would immediately be dispatched like a flash of lightning from his finger tip. As He would speak another angel would be dispatched like a flash from his mouth. Then as his gaze went in this direction and that other angels would be dispatched like laser beams from his eyes. The scene became one of great angelic activity. Then bit by bit I could see other columns of smoke beginning to rise and join the layer of cloud. Some were from individual believers exercising their priestly ministry, others were from church groups at prayer and worship. Gradually the cloud of God's presence began to thicken and there was a sense that the spiritual atmosphere was changing over the city and region.

That picture has stayed with me and seems to give me a sense of what is happening as we establish altars of prayer in our territory.

"The better we understand our part and God's part, often fulfilled by the angels as his agents, the better we are able to succeed in our assignment to take our territory for the Lord."

CHAPTER 9

Occupying our Assigned Territory

Abraham, Isaac and Jacob had fulfilled the first stage of God's plan to take the territory of Canaan. They had established the presence of God in the land. But they were still only a small family in a land occupied mainly by the Canaanite peoples. God had to turn them into a nation who could fully possess and occupy the land as owners. Abraham had never owned more than a field with a cave which he bought to bury his wife in.

Life can often take a strange turn of events, and within Jacob's lifetime the whole family of Abraham's descendants ended up outside their God-given territory because of famine. In Egypt they multiplied, at an alarming rate as far as the Egyptians were concerned, and were reduced to slavery. After 430 years God sent Moses to deliver them and bring them out into the territory God had promised to their fathers. He delivered them miraculously through the Red Sea and brought them to Sinai to teach them his ways and to enter into a covenant with them as a nation to be his people. He gave them their territorial assignment, complete with the boundaries and assurance of victory over the enemies who were still in the land.

And he began with the promise to send an angel ahead of them to guard, guide and lead them.

"See, I am sending an angel ahead of you to guard you along the way and to bring you to the place I have prepared. Pay attention to him and

listen to what he says. Do not rebel against him; he will not forgive your *rebellion, since my Name is in him. If you listen carefully to what he says* *and do all that I say, I will be an enemy to your enemies and will oppose* *those who oppose you. My angel will go ahead of you and bring you into* *the land of the Amorites, Hittites, Perizzites, Canaanites, Hivites and* *Jebusites, and I will wipe them out. Do not bow down before their gods* *or worship them or follow their practices. You must demolish them and* *break their sacred stones to pieces. Worship the LORD your God, and his* *blessing will be on your food and water. I will take away sickness from* *among you, and none will miscarry or be barren in your land. I will give* *you a full life span.*

I will send my terror ahead of you and throw into confusion every nation *you encounter. I will make all your enemies turn their backs and run.* *I will send the hornet ahead of you to drive the Hivites, Canaanites* *and Hittites out of your way. But I will not drive them out in a single* *year, because the land would become desolate and the wild animals too* *numerous for you. Little by little I will drive them out before you,* **until** **you have increased enough to take possession of the land***.*

I will establish your borders *from the Red Sea to the Mediterranean* *Sea, and from the desert to the Euphrates River. I will give into your* *hands the people who live in the land, and you will drive them out before* *you. Do not make a covenant with them or with their gods. Do not let* *them live in your land or they will cause you to sin against me, because the* *worship of their gods will be a snare to you."* Exodus 23:20-33 [NIVUK]

This angel had a very significant role to fulfil in bringing the people into their territory. His identity is not given but the expression *"My name is in him"* could mean either that God's name is included in the angel's name, or that he is an embodiment of God's person and character and is a periphrasis for the presence of God himself. If we take the former option it could refer to Michael, whose name includes El the name of God and means *"Who is like God?"* Since Michael is referred to in Daniel specifically as the prince of the people of Israel who watches over their territory, that may be a possibility.

However, on the whole, the second option is more likely and could therefore refer to a theophany of the pre-incarnate Christ. This viewpoint is reinforced if this is the same angel who manifested himself to Joshua as the Commander of the Lord's army when they had crossed the Jordan into the land. Certainly he speaks with God's authority as he has to be listened to and not rebelled against. The actual experience of God leading the nation through the wilderness was by God speaking from above the mercy seat to Moses in the tent of meeting. It was the cloud of Shekinah glory that led them. They were to move when the cloud moved and stop when the cloud stopped. Perhaps this Shekinah was the angel referred to. In any event the angel serves the purposes of God and carries out God's functions to lead, guide, direct, protect and bring them into their territory.

In this assignment to take their designated territory there are several key points to note.

- God had a specific *"place"* prepared for His people and it was the angel's assignment and responsibility to guard them en route and bring them to that place.

- Listening to the angel and obeying His instructions was to listen to God himself. If one rejects God's messenger one rejects the One who sent him.

- God gives 10 promises in this passage which parallel the 10 commandments given earlier. The book of the covenant, Exodus 20-23, begins with 10 commands and ends with 10 promises.

- The promises are conditional on fulfilling the commands.

- Worshipping the Lord was their central responsibility.

- They were to demolish the sacred stones and idolatrous objects in the land *after* God had wiped out their enemies.

- God would send terror and confusion to their enemies and make their enemies turn their backs and flee.

- God would use aspects of nature, such as hornets, to drive them out.

- God would use His people to drive them out as well.

- God would do it in stages and phases, only at the pace that they could occupy and consolidate the territory as their own.

- God would establish their borders so that they would eventually occupy all the territory assigned to them.

- But it was dependent on them fully following God's commands and moving forward to take their territory.

- God's blessings would be on their food and water. They would be blessed with no sickness, no miscarriages, no barrenness and no premature death! What promises!

Taking the Territory of One's Heart

It should also be noted that they had to take the territory of their own hearts first, before they could take territory from the enemy! That was what lay behind their initial refusal to enter after the 10 spies came back with a negative report about the problems they would face. In contrast to Abraham's faith in entering the land in obedience, *"they could not enter in because of unbelief."* Hebrews 3:19 *"We are warned against having a sinful unbelieving heart."* Hebrews 3:12.

During the 40 years subsequent wandering in the wilderness God was testing them to see what was in their heart.

*"Remember how the LORD your God led you all the way in the wilderness these forty years, to humble and **test you in order to know what was in your heart, whether or not you would keep his commands.** He humbled you, causing you to hunger and then feeding you with manna, which neither you nor your ancestors had known, **to teach you that man does not live on bread alone but on every word that comes from the mouth of the LORD**. Your clothes did not wear out and your feet did not swell during these forty years. Know then in your heart that as a man disciplines his son, so the LORD your God disciplines you."*
Deuteronomy 8:2-5

God wanted to see if they would obey him no matter what the circumstances. He wanted them to learn that spiritual life with all God's blessings comes by living by the Word of God. They needed to be dependant daily on what God said to them and live by that. If there was no water they were to trust God and God would provide water. If the water was bitter they were to seek God about the issue and do whatever God told them no matter how ridiculous that seemed. Normally throwing in some wood wouldn't cure undrinkable water, but if that was what God said to do then they needed to do it and live by that obedience.

If God said to strike the rock and water would come out to be enough for several million people and their flocks and herds, that was what they were to do, and they would live by obeying God's directions. If God said to speak to the rock then that would be sufficient. Even Moses missed that one and forfeited entry to the land himself because of it. God wanted to see what was in their heart whether they would obey God's word in faith or grumble about their problems. Like us so often, they grumbled and complained and rebelled against God and Moses and wanted to go back to their old life in slavery having forgotten just how bad that really was.

Radical Obedience

When we did the first leg of our prayer walk from Loop Head to Galway city, a distance of 96 miles which took 4 days, I felt that God's directions were the same as those Jesus gave to the disciples when he sent them out without money or food on their first assignment. We ate blackberries along the roadside, drank from streams or cattle troughs. We felt we were only free to ask people for a drink of water but not food, but we could accept food if it were offered. It was unusually hot weather for Ireland at the end of August and we slept in a farmer's hay barn or on someone's floor if we were offered shelter. We took no money with us and only the clothes we stood in. It seemed strange instructions in our sophisticated Western society. But we felt that obedience was important.

We made it for the first 2 days but, with all the physical exertion of walking, praying continuously along the roads, speaking with people we met, or preaching the Gospel in the open air at Kilkee strand, my energy and faith ran out. One of the team had to leave to go back to work the following morning so when we reached the town where he had left his car and money in preparation, the temptation to eat and take a break was too great for me, so I yielded. We took a day off, which was probably practical wisdom in the first place, and resumed the remainder the following day.

I learned that in discerning what God is saying it is also possible to make certain presumptions as to what that means. It is important to obey what God has clearly said because God's blessing attaches to that. But God hadn't specified the timeframe, that was my assumption and that overtaxed us. I also learned that even when we miss it, God still sees our heart and honours that. The second leg of that walk proved to be more fruitful in terms of connecting with people along the way. We visited a caravan of travelling people camping on the roadside and were welcomed. We were asked to pray for sick people. The children ran ahead of us shouting that *"holy men"* were coming. It proved to be an open door for the Gospel and in the subsequent season a substantial number of the travelling community in the region came to know the Lord. One of the keys to that was through healing miracles which really spoke to their community.

We need to take the ground of our hearts if we are to take any territory for God in the lives of others. This involves primarily coming to a place of obeying God's mandate for our lives at all costs. It involves feeding on the Word of God and living by the Word of God because the words that he speaks to us are spirit and life. It involves overcoming the fear of man and determining to be people of radical obedience. When a generation arose in Israel that were prepared to believe the promises and commands of God and cross over the Jordan to enter the promised land they discovered in effect that God was already ahead of them.

Joshua's Angel Encounter

"Now when Joshua was near Jericho, he looked up and saw a man standing in front of him with a drawn sword in his hand.

Joshua went up to him and asked, 'Are you for us or for our enemies?' 'Neither,' he replied, 'but as commander of the army of the LORD I have now come.' Then Joshua fell facedown to the ground in reverence, and asked him, 'What message does my Lord have for his servant?' The commander of the LORD's army replied, 'Take off your sandals, for the place where you are standing is holy.' And Joshua did so." Joshua 5:13-15.

God had promised that He would send His angel ahead of them to prepare the way and to bring them to the place He had prepared for them. Only when they arrived in the land does this angel now manifest in human form. He has the battle strategy for taking Jericho, the first city they were to conquer. It seems so often that we have to travel in faith, obey in faith, face obstacles in faith just believing and acting on what God has said, without any physical manifestation of

God's presence or angelic activity. God is God and chooses to do what He wants, when He wants, according to His wisdom. But isn't it great when He shows up!

The angel, or was it a pre-incarnate manifestation of Jesus, declares himself to be the Commander of the Lord's army. One of God's titles in Scripture is the Lord of Hosts, referring to the hosts of fighting angels who engage in spiritual warfare in the heavenly realms. God has 2 armies, the celestial army of warrior angels and the terrestrial army of His believing saints. Jesus is commander of both. Joshua was the human general who had to lead the ground troops while the angelic general provided air cover with His celestial army. The two needed to work together to take the territory. In modern warfare it is the aerial bombardments that do the damage, but it takes boots on the ground to occupy the territory and drive out the enemy. It is the angelic army that takes on our enemy and his troops but it is we who win the delivered people to the Lord and disciple them to be part of His kingdom on earth.

The strategy Joshua was given was a strange one if one were only thinking in human terms.

"Then the LORD said to Joshua, 'See, I have delivered Jericho into your hands, along with its king and its fighting men. March around the city once with all the armed men. Do this for six days. Have seven priests carry trumpets of rams' horns in front of the ark. On the seventh day, march around the city seven times, with the priests blowing the trumpets. When you hear them sound a long blast on the trumpets, have the whole army give a loud shout; then the wall of the city will collapse and the army will go up, everyone straight in." Joshua 6:2-5

It was not the earthly army of Joshua's troops who were going to make the wall fall down even with boots marching in unison with shouts and trumpets. It was the heavenly army who would ensure the walls fell down **into the ground**, not falling out or in, according to archaeologists. Then Joshua's army could walk straight in over the walls and take the city. The troops were engaged in spiritual warfare:

- Their vision was filled with a God-given picture, *"See, I have delivered Jericho into your hands, along with its king and fighting men"*. God had given them a word to believe and live by and fill their vision with.

- They were physically, and thereby spiritually marching around the city just as Abraham had walked around the whole land some 500 years previously.

- The priestly role was to the fore, as they carried the ark of the presence of God around the city each day in sustained priestly worship which is God's means of bringing in His kingdom.

- On the seventh day everything intensified as they marched around the city 7 times with the priests blowing trumpets. The sounding of trumpets in battle was akin to the 7 angels in Revelation 8 sounding the 7 trumpets to unleash the judgment of God on the earth. God's judgment on Jericho was announced all day.

- Then there was a final long blast which was the heavenly signal for the earthly regiment to shout in unison and in agreement with the sound in the heavens.

- At that the walls would fall down and the army would just walk straight in.

The collaboration of earth with heaven is key to taking the land. The initiative is from heaven and the response in from earth. We cannot do what only God can do, and he will not do what he has told us to do. We engage in our priestly ministry and release the angels to send fire on the earth. We preach the Gospel and lay hands on the sick in total faith that God will save and heal and demonstrate His kingdom by the power of the Holy Spirit. The better we understand our part and God's part, often fulfilled by the angels as His agents, the better we are able to succeed in our assignment to take our territory for the Lord.

Jericho is just one example. Every city had a different strategy and they had to listen to God for that strategy. The history of the nation of Israel is filled with examples of success and failure and these examples are given for us to learn from as we seek to take our own territory for the Lord. One of the key things we learn from the example of Jericho is the need for both of God's armies to work in concert. The *"air war"* of prayer, praise, intercession and doing prophetic acts in obedience is co-operating with the angels at the golden altar. This releases the angels to do a real demolition job on the enemy's air troops symbolised by hurling fire on the earth as heaven's bombs are unloaded on the enemy strongholds.

But boots on the ground are necessary to reap the harvest of souls released from the enemy's grip. We are mandated to proclaim the Good News of the kingdom of God and demonstrate the love and power of God through doing good and healing all who are oppressed by the enemy, like Jesus did. When Paul said that God's purpose was that we should be, *"conformed to the image of His Son"* he wasn't just referring to us developing Christlike character, important as that is. We are to do as Jesus did and that is described by Peter in Acts 10:38. *"God anointed Jesus of Nazareth with the Holy Spirit and power, and how he went around doing good and healing all who were under the power of the devil, because God was with him."*

So in addition to our House of Prayer, some of the young people are dedicated to going out into the streets to share the love and power of God with people. They are led by a young man who asks God for words of knowledge for people, then goes to the people God shows him and shares those words. They are often astounded and respond, *"how did you know that?"* That provides an opportunity to pray for people who are open and many are being touched by God in this way.

The Need for Spiritual Perception and Revelation

Prophetic perception of the spirit realm enables us to be more effective in collaborating with God and His angels. Lack of perception restricts our ability to function effectively in faith and leaves us more prone to fear. Elisha prayed that his servant's spiritual eyes would be opened to see the angelic army that was with them.

"When the servant of the man of God got up and went out early the next morning, an army with horses and chariots had surrounded the city. Oh no, my lord! What shall we do? the servant asked. Don't be afraid, the prophet answered. Those who are with us are more than those who are with them. And Elisha prayed, Open his eyes, LORD, so that he may see. Then the LORD opened the servant's eyes, and he looked and saw the hills full of horses and chariots of fire all around Elisha." 2 Kings 6:15-17

When seemingly insurmountable obstacles face us in taking our territory and we face setbacks and opposition we need to see things from God's perspective. We need revelation to stir faith and banish fear. The spiritual reality is that the angelic army with us is greater than the visible obstacles and the forces of darkness arrayed against us.

Discerning Deceiving Angels

One of the most subtle strategies of the enemy is to disguise himself as an angel of light.

"For such people are false apostles, deceitful workers, masquerading as apostles of Christ. And no wonder, for satan himself masquerades as an angel of light. It is not surprising, then, if his servants also masquerade as servants of righteousness." 2 Corinthians 11:13-15.

One of the battles Paul frequently faced was that satan tried to lure people away from the fullness of the Gospel he had preached. The evil one obviously wanted to re-take territory he had lost. One of his strategies was to inspire *"false apostles"* who were masquerading as apostles of Christ. Their most significant trait was pride, just like satan. They sought to set themselves up and tried to pull down the true servants of God. The church needed discernment to recognise false apostles and demonic angels masquerading as angels of light. One of the things God commended the church at Ephesus for was that they had tested and discerned those who claimed to be apostles but were imposters. [Revelation 2:2]

The Galatian churches had been bewitched into returning to trust in law observance rather than simple faith in Christ. [Galatians 3]. Paul was going through labour pains again to see them brought back to the Gospel of grace through faith. He warns them in the strongest possible terms.

"I am astonished that you are so quickly deserting the one who called you to live in the grace of Christ and are turning to a different gospel—which is really no gospel at all. Evidently some people are throwing you into confusion and are trying to pervert the gospel of Christ. But even if we or an angel from heaven should preach a gospel other than the one we preached to you, let them be under God's curse!" Galatians 1:6-8

Paul alerted them to the danger of being deceived by a demon, masquerading as an angel of light to preach a different Gospel. It's not the angels' assignment to preach the Gospel, so even that should get the warning lights going if someone recounts a different Gospel, claiming it to be from an angel. Paul warned the Thessalonians that in the last days there would even be counterfeit signs and wonders and miracles by the working of satan with the objective of deceiving, if possible, even genuine Christians.

"The coming of the lawless one will be in accordance with how satan works. He will use all sorts of displays of power through signs and wonders that serve the lie, and all the ways that wickedness deceives those who are

perishing. They perish because they refused to love the truth and so be saved." 2 Thessalonians 2:9-10

Their protection from deception would be their love of the truth, not just a fascination with the supernatural. God's word is the bulwark of truth to which we need to be unwaveringly committed.

In our contemporary post-modern Western world, the man in the street is not so committed to seeking the truth as to seeking experience. This leaves him vulnerable to all types of spiritual experience of a counterfeit nature, many claiming to have angelic encounters. There is a host of New Age literature about angels most of which falls into this category. Scripture warns us very clearly about the danger of being experience orientated rather than truth orientated. We need to make sure that our experiences of the spirit realm, including angels, is firmly in line with the revealed truth of Scripture. That is why I have sought in this book to base my understanding on what Scripture teaches.

Unfortunately, many who gained their first spiritual experience through the charismatic movement were never grounded in the full truth of the Word of God and became easy prey to this deception. Consequently many go in search of alleged angelic visitations and pursue the messages thus delivered, without checking if these messages correspond with the full truth of Scripture.

Understandably, in some ways, many in the Evangelical world, who are firmly committed to the truth, are sceptical about the spirit realm and any supernatural manifestations. This position, I would contend, is totally unbiblical. It is the Bible which gives us the only reliable information about angels and the whole spirit realm. Truth can also be experienced, and the supernatural nature of God and the Christian Gospel demand to be experienced supernaturally. The two are not mutually exclusive but reinforce each other.

"The angels assigned to us and our territory-taking mandate are more than all who are against us."

CONCLUSION

In conclusion, my prayer for everone committed to taking the territory God has assigned to them is the prayer Elisha prayed for his servant. ***"Open his eyes Lord so that he may see."*** The angels assigned to us and our territory-taking mandate are more than all who are against us. I pray the same prayer for myself as I continue to seek God for more revelation on how to know God better and how to fulfil my current mandate more effectively. I realise that I have only dipped my toe in the water, so to speak, in this realm. Like Paul, I do not consider that, *"I have yet laid hold of all that God has laid hold of me for, but I press on towards the goal to which God has called me."*

Paul considered that the prayer for a Spirit of wisdom and revelation was a priority prayer for the believers he cared for.

*"I keep asking that the God of our Lord Jesus Christ, the glorious Father, may give you the **Spirit of wisdom and revelation**, so that you may know him better."* Ephesians 1:17

It has got to be primarily about knowing God and pursuing a life of intimacy with him as David and Paul did. It's about loving God with all our soul, mind, will and strength, and loving our neighbour as ourself. It's not about angels per se, but only as they help us to know and serve God better in our primary calling. Yet we need to recognise how God operates in territorial terms, because angels are God's servants to help us take our territory.

BIBLIOGRAPHY

Deuteronomy by J.A. Thompson, Tyndale Old Testament Commentaries; *Published by Intervarsity Press.*

The Epistle to the Hebrews by F.F. Bruce, New International Commentary New Testament; *Published by Eerdmans*

Le réveil des Cévennes by Pierre Demaude L'histoire du mouvement prophétique des Huguenots; *Edition Réveille-toi*

Le théâtre sacré des Cévennes by Maximilien Misson; *Les éditions de Paris*

Les prophètes protestants by Ami Bost; *Edition des Lettres de Neff, Genève*

Angels: God's Secret Agents by Billy Graham; *Published by Doubleday Books*

Psalms 1-72 by Derek Kidner Tyndale Old Testament Commentaries; *Published by Intervarsity Press*

St Patrick's Confession; Duffy, Joseph, Patrick in his own words

Rees Howells Intercessor by Norman Grubb; *Published by Lutterworth Press, London*

prayforfrance.org

franceenfeu.com

Contact

To contact the author, see:
facebook.com/territorialangels

Or email:
info.harvestfrance@gmail.com

Visit our shop at:
www.harvestfrance.com

Also available in French:
«Les anges dans notre territoire»

www.laboitechretienne.com

Lookout for Graeme's next book

"The Companion Volume"

Inspired to write a book?

Contact

Maurice Wylie Media
Inspirational Christian Publisher

Based in Northern Ireland and distributing around the world.

www.MauriceWylieMedia.com

PERSONAL NOTES

PERSONAL NOTES

PERSONAL NOTES

PERSONAL NOTES

PERSONAL NOTES

Printed in Great Britain
by Amazon

81490492R00068